BACKROADS
OF ROUTE 66

BACKROADS OF

Route 66

YOUR GUIDE TO ADVENTURES AND SCENIC DETOURS

JIM HINCKLEY

motorbooks

Brimming with creative inspiration, how-to projects, and useful information to enrich your everyday life, quarto.com is a favorite destination for those pursuing their interests and passions.

Inspiring | Educating | Creating | Entertaining

First Published in 2022 by Motorbooks, an imprint of The Quarto Group,
100 Cummings Center, Suite 265-D, Beverly, MA 01915, USA.
T (978) 282-9590 F (978) 283-2742 Quarto.com

Motorbooks titles are also available at discount for retail, wholesale, promotional, and bulk purchase. For details, contact the Special Sales Manager by email at specialsales@quarto.com or by mail at The Quarto Group, Attn: Special Sales Manager, 100 Cummings Center, Suite 265-D, Beverly, MA 01915, USA.

26 25 24 23 22   1 2 3 4 5

ISBN: 978-0-7603-7449-8

Digital edition published in 2022
eISBN: 978-0-7603-7450-4

Library of Congress Cataloging-in-Publication Data

Names: Hinckley, Jim, 1958- author.
Title: The backroads of Route 66 : your guide to adventures and scenic
    detours / Jim Hinckley.
Other titles: Route 66 backroads.
Description: Beverly, MA : Motorbooks, an imprint of the Quarto Group,
    [2022] | Includes index. | Summary: "The Backroads of Route 66 explores
    the landmarks, natural wonders, and historical gems left to be explored
    off the beaten path of America's most famous byway"-- Provided by
    publisher.
Identifiers: LCCN 2021060846 | ISBN 9780760374498 (trade paperback) | ISBN
    9780760374504 (ebook)
Subjects: LCSH: United States Highway 66--Guidebooks. | West (U.S.)--Tours.
    | Scenic byways--West (U.S.)--Guidebooks. | Automobile travel--West
    (U.S.)--Guidebooks.
Classification: LCC F595.3 .H56 2022 | DDC 917.804--dc23/eng/20211220
LC record available at https://lccn.loc.gov/2021060846

Design: Kelley Galbreath

Printed in China

Acknowledgments

I CANNOT IMAGINE HOW IT WOULD BE POSSIBLE to transform an idea into a book without the support, encouragement, and insight of my dearest friend. For almost forty years, she has kept me focused, accompanied me on wild international adventures, and made sure that I didn't forget to eat during the push to meet deadlines.

The people who work tirelessly to keep the infectious spirit of Route 66 alive and preserve its landmarks also should be acknowledged. They have provided friendship, ideas, information, and encouragement.

And I would also like to say thank you to the contributors of photos. They have provided historical context by sharing their collections and different perspectives.

The editors also deserve some recognition. Often overlooked, they are the folks who work tirelessly behind the scenes to catch the author's mistakes and keep them from straying off topic or becoming long winded.

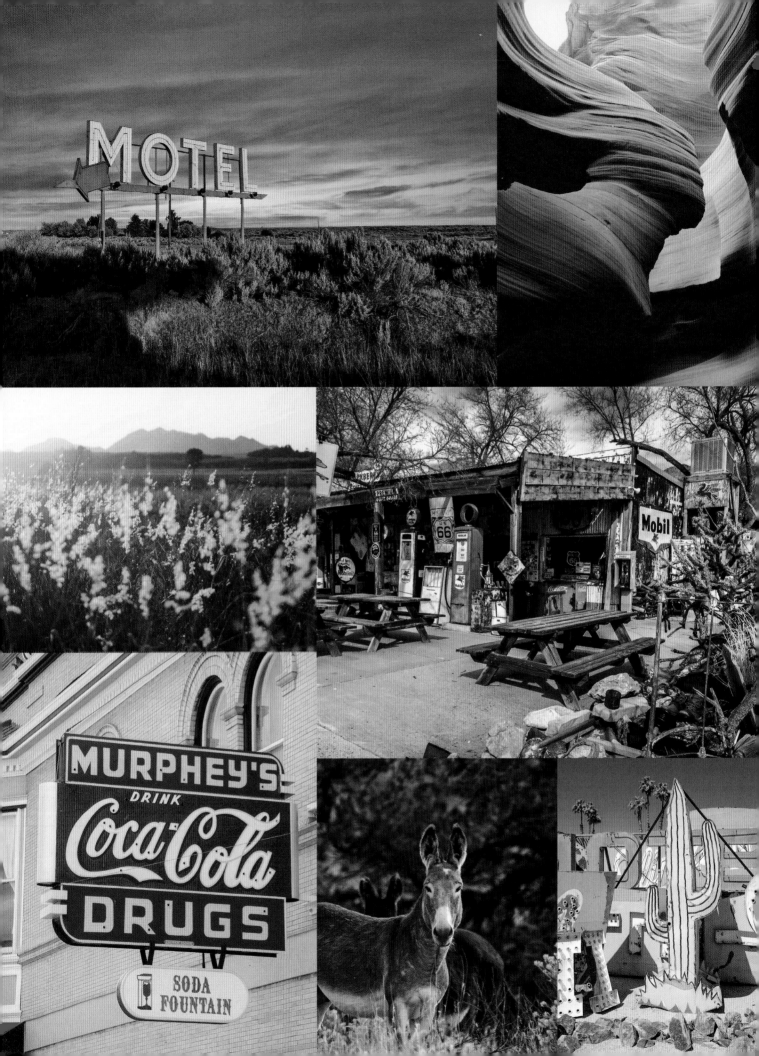

Contents

Introduction

ROUTE 66 IS NO MERE ROAD TRIP. It is the stuff of dreams, a magical place where the past, present, and even the future blend seamlessly.

Often, however, Route 66 enthusiasts get so caught up in their adventure they become myopic. As a result, they miss countless opportunities to enhance their adventure with scenic wonders, historic sites, time capsule restaurants, and towns that time has bypassed.

An argument could be made that Route 66 has inspired more ink to cover its praises than asphalt to pave it. Yet, little has been published about the wonders awaiting discovery via short detours on the backroads.

With a short side trip or loop drive, the very essence of the Route 66 experience is magnified. In Arizona, a detour of just a dozen miles (19.3 km) is all that is needed to escape the desert heat for the pine-forested oasis of Hualapai Mountain Park and enjoy fine dining at the historic Hualapai Mountain Lodge as elk graze outside the window.

From Peach Springs, Arizona, it is a scenic sixty mile (96.6 km) drive on Diamond Creek Road through Diamond Creek Canyon to the Colorado River. This is the only road that provides vehicular access to the bottom of the Grand Canyon.

Those sections of the original Route 66 alignment which still exist and haven't been displaced by interstates course through many of the country's most dynamic cities. But traffic congestion and crime, real and perceived, keep many enthusiasts from exploring the beginning or the end of the storied old highway. This also keeps them from discovering special places like the Petersen Automotive Museum or the century-old Grand Central Market.

The western terminus of the awe-inspiring Angel's Crest Highway, one of the most beautiful drives in America, is less than forty miles (64.4 km) from where Route 66 ends in California. In New Mexico, you can visit a wonderful little village that has been perched on a towering monolith of stone for almost a thousand years in the morning and be back on Route 66 in time for lunch at a diner that opened its doors in 1947.

Route 66 can also be the gateway to centuries of presidential history. The home of Abraham Lincoln is mere blocks from Route 66 in Springfield, Illinois. Harry Truman owned a mine in Commerce, Oklahoma. Theodore Roosevelt dedicated the Soldiers and Sailors Monument on Courthouse Square in Pontiac, Illinois, in 1903.

Scenic wonders are also a part of the Route 66 experience. Here, too, a detour on the backroads can enrich the adventure.

Cuba, Missouri, is home to the iconic Wagon Wheel Motel, the oldest continuously

operated motel on Route 66. A few miles (5 to 6 km) to the north on Highway 19 is the 19 Drive-In theater that opened in 1955. Follow this highway twenty miles (32.2 km) south and discover the majesty of Maramec Spring Park, proclaimed by the state tourism office as one of the top beauty spots in Missouri.

In between is Steelville, a town where time stopped years ago. Here, you will find Rich's Famous Burgers, a diner that opened in 1955, and the Spare Rib Inn that opened in 1929.

This book is a companion to essential guides such as the *EZ 66 Guide for Travelers* and the Route 66 Navigation app. This book is also your passport to adventures on the Main Street of America and the backroads of Route 66.

Part One
ILLINOIS

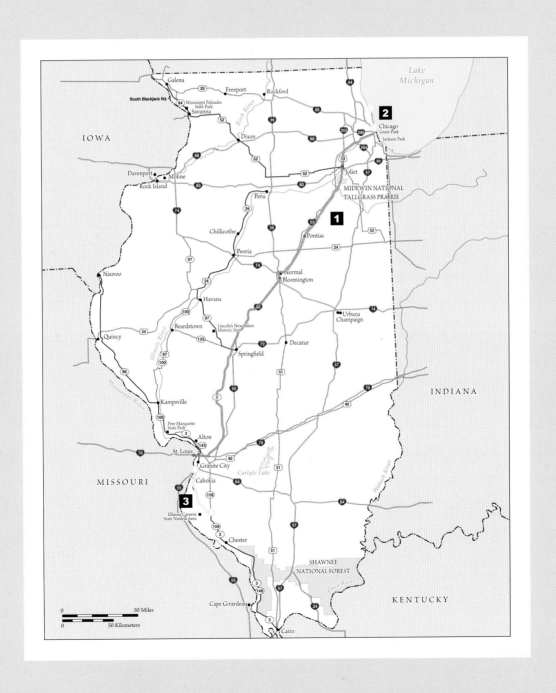

DRIVE ONE
ROUTE 66 IN
"THE LAND OF LINCOLN"

THE VIBRANT ATMOSPHERE THAT IS "the Loop" district and Lake Shore Drive in Chicago fill the traveler with an eager anticipation. And so, it is hard to imagine a better place for beginning a Route 66 adventure.

In Chicago, beginning in the 1950s, Route 66 followed two one-way corridors: Jackson Avenue and Adams Street. Jackson was the original alignment. It was also the course for one of the highway's predecessors, Trail to Sunset, an early automobile road connecting Chicago and Los Angeles established in 1910 by A. L. Westgard.

The original terminus of Route 66 was at the intersection of Jackson and Michigan Boulevard. The End Route 66 sign at this intersection has become a favored photo stop for enthusiasts. I prefer to commemorate the start of a westbound Route 66 trip with a photo at the post-1937 terminus at Lake Shore Drive.

If you are starting the odyssey in Chicago, I

ABOVE The original eastern terminus of Route 66 in Chicago shifted numerous times as the highway evolved.
PREVIOUS, LEFT A simple signpost in the heart of Chicago has become a destination for legions of Route 66 enthusiasts.

also recommend a hearty breakfast at Lou Mitchell's located at 565 West Jackson Boulevard. This iconic restaurant opened in 1923 and has become a traditional starting point for the Route 66 enthusiast. It has been operating at its current location since 1926.

A tradition for almost ninety years, all women and children receive free Milk Duds when they enter the restaurant in keeping with the hospitable Greek custom of offering sweets as a warm welcome. Milk Duds were the candy of choice because not only were they originally manufactured in Chicago, but also the owner of the company was a friend, and customer, of Lou Mitchell's.

If you have run the highway west to east, the best place to celebrate the end of your journey is The Berghoff at 17 West Adams Street. It opened in 1898 as a saloon for men only that offered a free sandwich with a nickel glass of beer. Specializing in authentic German dishes and superb traditional American favorites, this is one of the oldest continuously operated restaurants on Route 66.

To get the most from your Chicago visit, do some planning in advance with the tourism website Choose Chicago (www.choosechicago.com). I would also suggest a guided tour with author and historian David Clark, the illustrious "Windy City Warrior" (www.windycitywarrior.com).

Before putting the big city in the rearview mirror, get the ultimate Route 66 selfie at Willis Tower. Located at 233 South Wacker Drive, at 1,450 feet (113 m) the tower is the third tallest building in the Western Hemisphere. From the Skydeck's glass ledge box that extends more than four feet (1.2 m) from the building face, the views and photo opportunities are unparalleled.

Route 66 in Illinois was rerouted several times before it was decommissioned. It was then segmented by creation of the interstate

BELOW For Route 66 travelers in the 21st century, Lou Mitchell's has become the traditional place to start a westbound odyssey.

BOTTOM In the era of the Route 66 renaissance, many Route 66 enthusiasts celebrate their west to east adventure at this iconic restaurant.

highway. Fortunately, the state of Illinois has been a leader in sign placement that makes it relatively easy to find the old highway.

After leaving the historic heart of Chicago, Route 66 continued west on Ogden and then Joliet Road. This is a true opportunity to experience Route 66 as it was before the interstate highway, with traffic, and lots of it. There are also innumerable sights to see, wonderful opportunities for photographs, and vintage destinations such as Henry's Drive-In at 6031 Ogden Avenue in Cicero.

Dating to 1950, this restaurant's slogan is "It's A Meal In Itself." It continues to be a favorite for locals as well as Route 66 travelers, and the Chicago-style hot dogs consistently rate as some of the best in the metro area.

Another notable eatery is Dell Rhea's Chicken Basket in Willowbrook that has been serving travelers and locals since 1946.

The restaurant was the outgrowth of a gas station, garage, and small diner complex known for its fried chicken.

The latter alignment through Plainfield was largely decimated by I-55. The original alignment along Joliet Road through Romeoville signed as State Highway 53 is dotted with throwbacks like White Fence Farm.

Robert C. Hastert purchased this restaurant in September 1954. It has grown over the years to include several large dining rooms, a petting zoo, and a small museum with vintage automobiles. But Hastert's restaurant, which is still managed by his family, has origins in a small diner that opened at this site in the 1920s.

In Romeoville, the Isle a la Cache Museum illustrates why this highway is often referenced as the crossroads of the past, present, and future. The museum is the centerpiece of a 101-acre (40.9 ha) riparian

CLOCKWISE FROM LEFT Illinois has become a leader in sign placement along Route 66 that officially ceased to exist as a U.S. highway nearly 40 years ago.

Serving locals and travelers since 1946, this restaurant illustrates why Route 66 is often referred to as a string of living time capsules.

In Romeoville, the Isle a la Cache forest preserve and museum is a window into the Illinois wilderness of the 18th century.

island and forest preserve with a trail system on the Des Plaines River. The museum transports the visitor to the eighteenth century when this location was a crossroads for Native American trade routes. Also on display are immersive exhibits about the area's rich natural history.

In the 1940s, several four-lane alignments were built to bypass urban congestion. But generally, Route 66 followed Highway 53 to Springfield. Then, south of Springfield, the latter alignment of Route 66 runs parallel to I-55, except for the 1950s alignment that passes through Collinsville.

The earliest alignment followed what is today State Highway 4. But here, too, there can be some confusion as the highway was rerouted in various towns over the years.

From Chicago to St. Louis, Route 66 courses across the heartland of Illinois for almost three hundred miles (482.8 km). Each town along Route 66 in Illinois has a special charm and unique attractions.

In Joliet, there is the Rialto Square Theatre, built in 1926. Intricate plasterwork, ornate ceilings, an historic organ, and other period features make the Rialto an architectural masterpiece. But what really sets this theatre apart are the thirty-two chandeliers, the largest of which is dubbed "the Duchess." Weighing 2.5 tons (2.3 mt) and measuring 22 feet (6.7 m), it is one of the largest crystal chandeliers in the country.

Apart from the metropolitan areas of Bloomington, Normal, and Springfield, the old highway in Illinois is lined with farms, agriculture, evidence of more than a century of mining, and forests. Along the way, charming communities that epitomize small-town America with fascinating museums and poignant memorials are tangible links to almost two centuries of history.

In Wilmington, there is the Launching Pad with its iconic Gemini Giant where, since the

early 1960s, good food and a unique photo opportunity have encouraged travelers to make a pit stop. The neglected Eagle Hotel, purportedly the oldest commercial building along Route 66 in Illinois dating to the mid-1830s, is located a few blocks away.

For Route 66 enthusiasts, the city of Braidwood is associated with the Polk-a-Dot Drive In. This classic diner, established in 1956, serves up good old-fashioned burgers in an atmosphere of absolute whimsy.

A tour of the Rialto Square Theater in Joliet, or attending a performance in this historic movie palace, will enhance a Route 66 odyssey.

It started out as a fast-food stand in a converted polka dot–covered school bus!

Gardner has transformed an ancient two-cell jail into an attraction that draws legions of international Route 66 enthusiasts eager to take a selfie behind bars. And it's also where you will find a monument to World War II hero Reverend Christian Christiansen. In Odell, there is the Standard Oil Gas Station, also called the Odell Station, built in 1932. It now serves as a visitor center.

In the era of Route 66 renaissance, Pontiac has become a model of historic district revitalization. The Old Log Cabin Restaurant opened in 1926 is still serving good meals and hot coffee. In Downtown Pontiac, colorful murals mimic vintage advertisements and present a sense of timelessness.

Surrounding the square dominated by the Livingston County Courthouse, built in 1875, are repurposed buildings with restaurants and an array of shops. They also house attractions such as the Pontiac-Oakland Museum and Research Center, the Museum of the Gilding Arts (MOGA), and Illinois Route 66 Association Hall of Fame & Museum.

In Chenoa, the Chenoa Pharmacy, opened in 1889, is an unusual but intriguing attraction. In Lexington, an abandoned section of the highway has been transformed into a walking trail known as Memory Lane that replicates the 1940s American roadside

CLOCKWISE FROM TOP LEFT The old Eagle Hotel in Wilmington is another example of the how the past and present blend seamlessly along Route 66.

The Log Cabin Inn in Pontiac is a tangible link to the infancy of Route 66 and the U.S. highway system.

The restoration of the Odell Station built in 1932 is but one manifestation of the small village's pride in connection with Route 66.

complete with vintage billboards and Burma Shave signs.

Buried but not lost among the modern urban landscape of Bloomington are finds such as the 1903 Old McLean County Courthouse, now home to the McLean County Museum of History, a museum that includes exhibits chronicling Abraham Lincoln's association with the city. This city is also home to the BEER NUTS factory, a family-owned business supplying those familiar, red-skinned nuts since the 1930s. A fascinating tour that culminates with some BEER NUT tasting is a must.

A bit over a dozen miles (19.3 km) south of Bloomington is a true national treasure, a roadside stop that has been serving travelers for more than a century, Funks Grove. This historic farm nestled among a natural stand of maples and ancient white oaks has been

doling out pure maple syrup since 1824. Located within Funks Grove is Funks Grove Nature Preserve, an eighteen-acre (7.3 ha) tract that is one of the largest areas of virgin forest remaining in Illinois. It was protected by the Funk family for 160 years.

In McLean, the Dixie Truckers Home opened its doors in 1928, making it the oldest continuously operated truck stop in America. And then there is Atlanta, a city that describes itself as "Very Small. Very Friendly. Very Route 66." It's filled with historic sites and unique attractions including The Hawes Grain Elevator, the only operational wooden grain elevator in the state.

Lincoln is the only community named for Abraham Lincoln before he became president. He was the attorney that platted and submitted the filing for the township. Near the historic depot is a monument that

ABOVE, LEFT In the shadow of the city's historic courthouse, the Pontiac Oakland Auto Museum is one of several world-class museums in Pontiac.

ABOVE, RIGHT Diminutive Atlanta, in the era of Route 66 renaissance, has morphed into a delightful blending of history and whimsy.

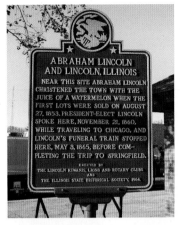

commemorates where Abraham Lincoln, according to legend, christened the site with the juice of a cut watermelon.

Also in Lincoln, at 914 5th Street, is a replica of the Postville Courthouse, now a state historic site. The town of Postville was established by Russell Post in late 1834 and served as the Logan County seat until 1847. While riding the Eighth Judicial Court circuit, Abraham Lincoln argued numerous cases in this courthouse.

After relocation of the county seat, the building was converted into a private residence. In 1929, it was purchased by Henry Ford, dismantled, and rebuilt in his Greenfield Village Museum complex located in Dearborn, Michigan.

To celebrate the town's centennial, using measurements taken from the original courthouse, this reproduction was constructed in 1953 on the original site. The first floor consists of an exhibit gallery and a reception room. The second floor is used for displays that represent an 1840's courtroom.

Lincoln College at 1115 Nicholson Road is home to the Lincoln Heritage Museum. Originally chartered as Lincoln University in 1865, ground for the first building was broken on President Lincoln's last birthday.

The keystone for the museum, established in 1942, was the donation of Judge Lawrence Stringer's expansive private collection of original materials pertaining to Lincoln and his association with Logan County. Robert Todd Lincoln Beckwith, the last surviving direct descendant of Abraham Lincoln, also donated a large collection of Abraham Lincoln artifacts.

ABOVE, LEFT Monuments commemorate the legend that Abraham Lincoln christened the townsite with watermelon juice, and his association with the community.

ABOVE, RIGHT Built in 1953, this is a replica of the Postville Courthouse in which Abraham Lincoln argued cases while traveling the Eighth Judicial Court circuit.

Exhibits include hundreds of rare photographs and objects including Civil War maps. The upstairs galleries provide a fully immersive experience that includes audio-video presentations and detailed nineteenth-century room recreations, including a haunting reproduction of the boarding-house room where President Lincoln died.

As the capital of Illinois since 1837, Springfield is a veritable treasure trove of history, from sites associated with President Lincoln to the famed Cozy Dog Drive In. Located at the Illinois State Fairgrounds is the Route 66 Experience developed by the Illinois Route 66 Scenic Byway. This unique exhibit introduces visitors to communities and attractions in the state along Route 66 from Chicago to the Chain of Rocks Bridge.

On Route 66, at 112 North Sixth Street in Springfield, the Abraham Lincoln Presidential Library and Museum transports the visitor back to the time of President Lincoln. Artifacts including personal effects, detailed exhibits, and state-of-the-art special effects blend seamlessly for an immersive experience.

On the corner of Tenth Street and Monroe is the Great Western Depot, also known as the Lincoln Depot, where Lincoln boarded the train for his journey to Washington, D.C. The most recent renovation in 2013 included the addition of a self-guided museum on the first floor.

At Sixth and Adams Street are the Lincoln-Herndon Law Offices. This historic building has been refurbished with such attention to detail there is a sense that Lincoln will be returning at any moment.

The only home Lincoln ever owned stands at the corner of Eighth and Jackson Street. Built in 1839, the modest home is the focal point of a four-block historic park that has been renovated to appear as it did in the years just prior to the American Civil War. Attention to detail, including placement of personal items belonging to Lincoln and his family, give a tour of the home an intimate feel.

A few blocks north at 1500 Monument Avenue, the somber Lincoln Tomb towers over his final resting place. It casts long shadows over the scenic and historic Oak Ridge Cemetery.

From Springfield to the Route 66 Mississippi River crossings, the storied highway has two distinctly different personalities. The original alignment follows State Highway 4 through charming old towns rich in history. Much of the post-1930 alignment has been erased by I-55 or serves as that highway's access road.

BELOW The attention to detail as well as placement of personal effects give a tour of Abraham Lincoln's home an intimate feel.

BOTTOM A tour through the home of Abraham Lincoln, and a stroll through the meticulously recreated neighborhood, transports the visitor to the era of mid-19th century.

There is a sense of timelessness when traveling the original alignment. From the hand-laid brick paving near Auburn to the town square in Carlinville, the infectious magic of Route 66 is made manifest at every turn.

The latter alignment has charm as well, but it has been tainted by its association with the interstate highway. Still, scattered here and there are delightful rarities such as the Ariston Cafe in Litchfield. The café opened on the square in Carlinville in 1924. After realignment of the highway, the current restaurant was built in 1935. It remained a one family–owned restaurant until 2018. Some furnishings date to a post–World War II remodel, and the restaurant appears the same as it did in the late 1940s.

The last miles of Route 66 in the Land of Lincoln are a confusing maze of alignments in an increasingly urban area. Jerry McClanahan, author of *EZ 66 Guide for Travelers*, says, "Route 66 evolved a bewildering tangle of 'main' and 'city' routes to cross into Missouri, many of which are difficult or not tourist friendly."

And that takes us to Mississippi River crossings. Before selecting a route into St. Louis, I suggest a walk across the river on the Chain of Rocks Bridge with its quirky twenty-two-degree bend at mid-river. Accessed via Exit 3A on I-270 west of Mitchell, this bridge built in 1929 was signed as an alternate Route 66 corridor, a beltline bypassing the city.

Featured in the 1981 film *Escape from New York*, the bridge was incorporated into the Trailnet network after its renovation as a pedestrian and bicycle bridge. With the unfortunate notoriety as an area prone to car break-ins, it is advised that travelers secure all items in the trunk before leaving to explore the bridge.

DRIVE TWO
THE CHICAGO COAST

THIS ROUTE 66 SIDE TRIP BEGINS WITH the urban oasis that is Calumet Beach Park. It continues along the shore of Lake Michigan, past Steelworkers Park, Rainbow Beach Park, and the South Shore Cultural Center to Jackson Park. Close by to this park is the Museum of Science and Industry.

The main building is the former Palace of Fine Arts built for the 1893 World's Columbian Exposition. The actual museum opened in 1933 during the Century of Progress Exposition. The diverse collection of exhibits provides something of interest for all age groups. Simulators as well as intriguing exhibits and dioramas chronicle the evolution of transportation over the course of centuries. The Transportation Gallery houses a detailed replica of the Wright brother's airplane flown in 1903, a Boeing 727, and historic locomotives. But the museum is not focused just on the past as evidenced by a recent exhibit featuring an assortment of pioneering technology entitled, *Fast Forward . . . Inventing the Future.*

ABOVE Lake Shore Drive with its string of parks presents the impression that Chicago is a coastal city rather than one located in the American Midwest.

The drive north is through a series of lakeside parks that provide stark contrast to the towering cityscape that dominates the western horizon. Museum Campus Drive courses through Burnham Park, 12th Street Beach, and Northerly Island Park and provides access to several "must-see" attractions.

What began as a permanent residence for the artifacts from the Columbia Exposition of 1893 transformed into the Field Museum of Natural History and is now one of the greatest museums of natural history in the world. The collection has grown to proportions befitting its prize exhibit, SUE—the largest and most complete Tyrannosaurus Rex skeleton in the world.

The second museum in the complex is the Adler Planetarium and Astronomy Museum. When its doors opened in 1930, this was the first planetarium in the western hemisphere.

On opening day, May 30, 1930, the John G. Shedd Aquarium was the largest aquarium in the world. An array of innovative exhibits presents a microcosm of aquatic environments ranging from the oceans and Great Lakes to the Amazon River and the Caribbean.

As Lake Shore Drive continues north, it hugs the lakeshore and traverses the green expanses of Grant Park near the western terminus of Route 66. Designated Lake Park in 1844 and renamed for President Ulysses S. Grant in 1901, this is one of the oldest parks in the city. Befitting that status is the majestic Buckingham Fountain built in 1927, featured in the opening credits for the 1990s television program *Married . . . with Children.*

Remarkably, a monument to President Abraham Lincoln stands in Grant Park, and in Lincoln Park, there is a monument to President Grant. The Art Institute of Chicago is located a few blocks away. Founded in 1879, it is one of the oldest and largest art galleries in the United States.

After crossing the Chicago River, take a turn east on West Illinois Street to Navy Pier, a Chicago landmark. Established as

Municipal Pier in 1916 as a shipping and recreational focal point for the city, it was renamed Navy Pier in 1927. The name change was a tribute to U.S. Navy personnel housed at the pier during training in World War I.

Extensive renovation of the complex commenced in 1994. With its amusement park, Chicago Shakespeare Theater, and Chicago Children's Museum, the pier has become a premier attraction in the city.

The next stop on the northward drive on Lake Shore Drive is Lincoln Park. Chicago's largest public park, with a shoreline stretching for seven miles (11.3 km), is full of activities and attractions, including the Lincoln Park Zoo, the Lakefront Trail, North Avenue Beach, Chicago History Museum, Theater on the Lake, and the Lincoln Park Conservatory.

The drive continues along the lakeshore, past Belmont Harbor, and through another string of parks. For those unfamiliar with the "Windy City," this drive serves as an introduction to all that makes Chicago one of the most beautiful cities in America.

With its stunning skyline as a backdrop, the drive along the lake shore in Chicago is a unique urban experience.

THIS ADVENTURE BEGINS WITH Cahokia Mounds State Historic Site, a vestige from the largest urban settlement of the Mississippian culture yet discovered. More than one thousand years before the arrival of Europeans, this was the largest city in a linked network of communities that covered most of present-day East St. Louis, Illinois, and St. Louis, Missouri, and the surrounding area.

Preserved at this site is the central section of a city estimated to be larger than London, England, was in 1250 CE. Designated a UNESCO World Heritage Site, there are more than fifty mounds of various types, excavated residential and public areas, and a reconstructed palisade using original post holes. Dominating the site is Monks Mound, the largest prehistoric earthen structure north of Mexico.

As a testimony to the advanced society that built this city, archeologists have excavated an astronomical observatory. The discovery of construction methods that were utilized are

ABOVE This artist rendering as a mural provides a glimpse into the lost world of the people who once called Cahokia home.

also indicative of the civilization's engineering skills.

Administered by the Illinois Historic Preservation Division, during the Illinois bicentennial, Cahokia Mounds was designated as one of the state's 200 Great Places by the American Institute of Architects. Numerous prestigious travel guides list this as a top attraction in Illinois.

The interpretive center is designed to provide an in-depth, detailed overview of the site and Mississippian culture. It also provides insight into the scope of the city and satellite communities' expansive reach in the river valley.

At its peak, a trade network connected Cahokia with villages throughout the central and southeastern United States and possibly in the Great Plains. Additional vestiges are the Starr Village and Mound Group archaeological site near Edwardsville about forty-five miles (72.4 km) north.

Before leaving Highway 3 and setting out across a timeless landscape of forests and farms on Highway 7, Maeystown Road, take some time to explore Waterloo. This charming village that can trace its beginnings to 1780 is a delightful blend of historic and modern.

This was the second American settlement in what was the Northwest Territory, and it was the first in Illinois. One of Waterloo's three notable museums awaiting discovery is Bellefontaine House. This historic home sits at the site of the town's original settlement and is operated by the Monroe County Historical Society.

The entire Waterloo Historic District is a recommended stop on the Kaskaskia-Cahokia Trail (KCT) route along Highway 3 from Cahokia. Archeological evidence indicates that portions of this trail were in use at least eight thousand years ago. It was a primary route for early European explorers

and settlers. Maps of the trail and a list of recommended sites are available at The Kaskaskia-Cahokia Trail website (www.kctrailillinois.org/maps). Compared to the KCT, Maeystown could almost be considered contemporary, founded in 1852. Yet, it has been listed on the National Register of Historic Places since 1978.

The well-preserved buildings built between the mid-1850s and 1910 were but one reason for the designation. Until 1943, residents preserved their German heritage by

The view from the summit of Monks Mound in the ancient city of Cahokia seems to blur the line between past and present.

conducting city business and church services in German.

Jacob Maeys, an immigrant from Bavaria, selected the site as the hills protected the village from river flooding and spring-fed streams provided adequate water for a mill. He was soon joined by German immigrants of the 1848 Movement, a group that fled their homeland for political and economic reasons.

Stone was the material of choice when the town was built. The bridge that serves as the entrance to the town was built of stone more than 140 years ago. The church, the mill, and walls bordering fields were all built of stone. And, it is claimed that Maeystown has the longest hand-laid stone street gutters in the United States, more than four hundred feet (121.9 m).

With a population of fewer than 175 people, there is something else that makes this town incredibly special. About thirty years ago, it was almost a complete ghost town, a forgotten place marooned on the backroads.

A group of friends from the St. Louis area discovered the village and began purchasing property. They then set about the restoration of homes, businesses, and historic infrastructure such as the gutters. Recently, the State of Illinois designated Maeystown "one of the best-preserved historic nineteenth- century towns in Illinois."

You can immerse yourself in the old-world experience with a stay at the Corner George Inn Bed & Breakfast. Built in 1884, this building was used as a hotel and saloon for decades.

There are only six original rooms, each out-fitted with antiques that enhance the sense of going back in time. But there are also modern amenities including a special whirlpool and loft suite. A breakfast of locally grown fruit and fresh eggs is served upstairs in a former meeting hall that was also used as a dancehall.

The business district is minuscule, and most stores, like the Maeystown General Store, which was the old 1904 general

CLOCKWISE FROM TOP LEFT Maeystown is a unique slice of history, as the entire town was listed on the National Register of Historic Places in 1978.

Dating to the years before the American Civil War, this historic stone bridge is a fitting portal to the classic town that is Maeystown.

The charm of Maeystown is best discovered by walking its quaint and quiet streets with hand-laid stone gutters.

mercantile, are only open on weekends or during festivals. This includes restaurants and coffee shops. Still, dining in Maeystown is another unique experience.

Hank and Lilly's Creekside Bar and Grill was a delicious surprise. On certain days, they offer takeout meals, ideal for a picnic along the creek. Other dining options usually require a short drive to Waterloo.

Festivals are as unique as Maeystown. The diversity, the vibrancy, and the authentic cultural experience will enhance your visit. A complete list of events is available on the village's website (https://maeystown.com/events/).

The first Sunday in May is Fruehlingsfest or Springfest. This event is a blending of antique fair and flower shows. Before COVID-19, this was one of the largest antique shows in southern Illinois. And of course, there is a lot of food with an emphasis on authentic German offerings.

The second Sunday in October is Oktoberfest, held in the meadows at the old bridge and mill. It is a wonderfully vibrant event with rug weavers, blacksmiths, wood workers, and artisans. And of course, there are traditional foods and fall drinks.

Popular nineteenth-century foods include turtle soup, kartoffelpuffer (potato pancakes), and kettle-cooked popcorn. There are also ample offerings of bratwurst, apple butter churned and cooked in iron kettles over an open fire, and lots of pies.

BELOW, FROM TOP Charming shops and restaurants encourage the visitor to slow the pace and simply savor the magic that is Maeystown.

The owner's pride of ownership at the Corner George Inn is made manifest in personal touches that instantly make the guest feel at home.

The Corner George Inn is a delightful 19th-century time capsule restored with an attention to detail and the needs of the modern traveler in mind.

Part Two
MISSOURI

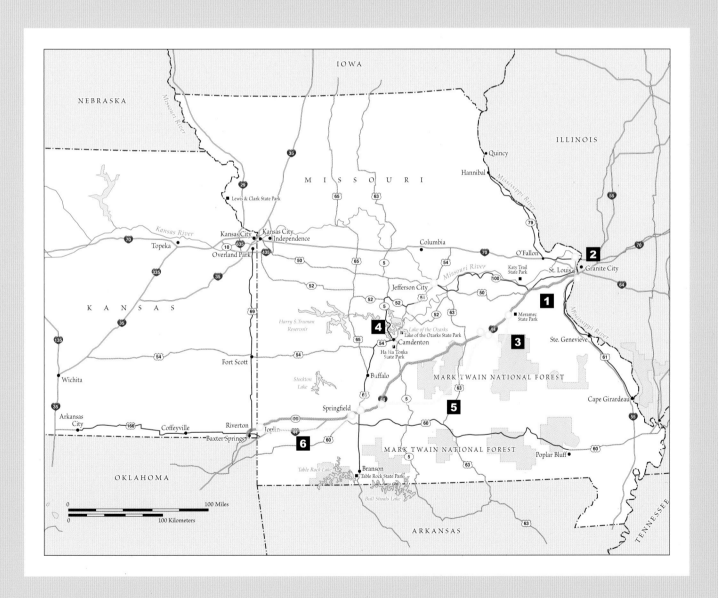

DRIVE ONE
ROUTE 66 IN "THE SHOW-ME STATE"

IN THE MODERN ERA, ROUTE 66 HAS often been described as a living time capsule. A more apt descriptor would be that it is a string of living time capsules. Nowhere is this more evident than in Missouri, "The Show-Me State."

In the city of St. Louis, Route 66 was aligned numerous times. Even the Mississippi River crossings were changed often. Jerry McClanahan, author of *EZ 66 Guide for Travelers*, sums it up succinctly: "St. Louis, gateway to the west, nests in a tangled web of roads and freeways. Over the decades U.S. 66 used a bewildering variety of streets thru the region."

The array of attractions, museums, and historic sites in St. Louis is almost overwhelming. As the city is the focus of Drive Two in this section, we will skip to Kirkwood on the western outskirts.

There are two distinctly different alignments of Route 66 west of St. Louis. Originally, the

ABOVE The historic heart of St. Clair with the Lewis Cafe is a charming area from mid-20th-century America.
PREVIOUS, LEFT The roots of the iconic Munger Moss Motel date to the establishment of a sandwich shop in 1936 along Route 66 at Devil's Elbow.

highway followed what is today Highway 100 through Manchester, Ballwin, and Fox Creek. The latter alignment is intertwined with I-44. Both alignments converge near Villa Ridge.

Almost as soon as you leave the city, the highway begins climbing into the Ozark Mountains. From this point on, the mountains define the Route 66 experience as the highway follows the contours of the land to Joplin, near the Kansas state line.

Both alignments are amply seasoned with legacies from the highway's glory days. But I prefer the later alignment through Pacific, a little town that figured prominently in the important but obscure 1864 Battle of Pacific during the American Civil War.

This alignment also bisects Route 66 State Park even though you cannot drive the highway through the park. The decking for the

Meramec River U.S. 66 Bridge was removed years ago, making it impossible to cross, but leaving a haunting image for a photograph.

The Route 66 State Park Visitor Center and museum are housed in the old Bridgehead Inn built in 1935. The opposite side of the Meramec River, across from the visitor center, is ideally suited for camping, fishing, hiking, bicycling, or just a pleasant picnic.

Around the downtown park in St. Clair is a perfect example of the time capsule reference to Route 66. The Lewis Cafe at 145 South Main Street opened in 1938. Stepping through the doors is like stepping back in time.

Just a few miles (5 to 6 km) south of Stanton is the one and only Meramec Caverns, a quintessential roadside attraction. For almost a century, the caverns have been marketed by

CLOCKWISE FROM LEFT
Built in 1910, the McKinley Bridge was one of several bridges used to carry Route 66 traffic across the Mississippi River.

Control of Pacific, an important railroad junction located on the Wire Road, was crucial for both Confederate and Union forces during the American Civil War.

Removal of the decking from the 1932 Route 66 Bridge left Route 66 State Park bisected by the Meramec River.

MERAMEC CAVERNS
"The 4-Story Wonder"   STANTON, MO.

MISSOURI'S LARGEST *ELECTRIC LIGHTED* CAVE
. . . World's only drive-in cave. Room for 300 cars.

linking them to stunning natural beauty, myth, urban legend, and history.

In 1949, when J. Frank Dalton, purported to be one hundred years old, claimed to be Jesse James living under an alias, it made news. To capitalize on a local legend that linked Jesse James with the caverns, Lester Dill, the cavern's owner, built a home for Dalton and relocated him to the site so he could spend the days telling tall tales to tourists.

But Dill did not stop there. He acquired an ancient log cabin, had it dismantled, and then rebuilt in the cavern. A new promotion was launched that centered on the discovery of Jesse James's hideout in Meramec Caverns.

The revitalization of Route 66 has inspired young entrepreneurs. In Sullivan, Missouri, Rich Dinkela, president of the Route 66 Association of Missouri, and his wife Christina, recently purchased the long-closed Shamrock Court with its stylish stonework from a family that owned it since the early 1950s. When they announced a cleanup weekend, volunteering Route 66 enthusiasts came from as far away as South Carolina.

The charming village of Cuba is a microcosm of everything that gives Route 66 an infectious allure. Visitors are often greeted as if they were old friends. The renovated Wagon Wheel Motel, which opened in the mid-1930s, artfully blends the property's historic detail with modern-day amenities.

Next door is Missouri Hick Bar-B-Que, a contemporary restaurant that presents the illusion of being as old as the highway out front. The specialty is traditional Ozark

CLOCKWISE, FROM LEFT Meramec Caverns has evolved as a tourist attraction since its entrance was used as a dance hall in the late 19th century.

The legend of Meramec Caverns' association with Jesse James became the cornerstone for a successful marketing campaign that helped make it a destination for Route 66 travelers.

The long-shuttered Shamrock Court in Sullivan, Missouri, is another Route 66 time capsule that is being given a new lease on life.

favorites, from their signature brisket to St. Louis–style ribs and more than fifteen sides including German potato salad and macaroni and cheese.

Shelly's, a small traditional diner where the locals, including the police, often gather for a hearty breakfast, is a few blocks to the west. And the 19 Drive-In theater, located on Highway 19, is still going strong after more than sixty years of operation.

At every turn in downtown Cuba there are colorful murals depicting scenes from the town's history. The city's innovative mural program led to recognition from the state and designation as "Route 66 Mural City."

On Main Street, one block off of Washington Street (Route 66), buildings dating to the late nineteenth century house wonderful

dining options: the colorful Riviera Maya Mexican Restaurant, with its truly unique décor and authentic Mexican food, and Frisco's Grill & Pub.

West of Cuba, Route 66 runs parallel to I-44. This presents an interesting contrast, and as is often the case on Route 66, that blurs the line between past and present. This is enhanced with roadside businesses and attractions such as the Fanning 66 Outpost with the country's second largest rocking chair, The Route 66 Red Rocker, and the 4M Vineyards & Farms roadside stand.

Each town, village, and hamlet offers an opportunity to experience Route 66 as it was in the pre-interstate highway era. And some, such as the ghost town of Arlington marooned on a truncated alignment of

STONYDELL SWIMMING POOL   ARLINGTON, MO.

Route 66, provide insight to the devastation wrought in small rural communities when the highway was bypassed.

At Exit 176, there is a short side trip along a forlorn segment of Route 66 that dead ends at the Little Piney River and the ghost town of Arlington that I highly recommend. Along the old highway, you will find the long-closed Vernelle's Motel and the ruins of John's Modern Cabins, originally Bill and Bess's Place, nestled in the woods.

Bill and Beatrice Bayliss established Bill and Bess's Place a few miles (5 to 6 km) west of Rolla in about 1931. It was a popular roadhouse with six small rustic cabins. John Dausch, who had purchased the property in 1950, closed the business around 1970 as the highway bypass had decimated business. After his death in 1971, the site was abandoned.

Arlington, with its defunct general store and abandoned century-old hotel, is an evocative site. Dating to the 1860s, the town is linked to a momentous Route 66 event. It was here that state highway workers celebrated completion of the paving of Route 66 in Missouri on January 5, 1931. The celebration included tossing coins into the wet concrete.

On the west side of the river, accessed from Exit 172 on Highway D, are the last fragments of the Stony Dell Resort, as well as a weathered old store and tumbledown cabins.

Nearby is the prized folk-art piece that is known as Larry Baggett's Trail of Tears Memorial. After years of abandonment and neglect, the site was restored and renamed Trail of Tears Memorial and Herbal Garden.

Encapsulated at Hooker Cut and Devil's Elbow is the entire evolution of Route 66. In 1941, the state of Missouri deemed Devil's Elbow "One of the Seven Beauty Spots of Missouri." Built in 1923, the steel-truss

CLOCKWISE FROM LEFT Less than a dozen miles (19.3 km) west of Rolla are the fading vestiges of John's Modern Cabins that opened in 1931 as Bill and Bess's Place.

Marooned at the end of a truncated alignment of the old highway are remnants of the ghost town of Arlington that dates to the 1860s.

The Stony Dell Resort complex built in 1932 by George Pruitt had a hotel, swimming pool, cabins, and a restaurant, but only ruins remain in the forest.

bridge over the Big Piney River has carried Ozark Trails Highway and Route 66 traffic. The Elbow Inn Bar & BBQ is an authentic roadhouse that opened in the 1930s.

The narrow road and bridge and sharp curves were a bottleneck for traffic by 1940. These problems were magnified with commencement of the construction of the U. S. Army training installation Fort Leonard Wood. And so, Hooker Cut was built as a bypass.

At the time of construction, it was the deepest highway cut in the United States. This was the first four-lane segment of Route 66 in Missouri. And it was the last segment of Route 66 to be bypassed in Missouri with completion of I-44.

Near St. Robert is a modern incarnation of the classic roadside attraction, Uranus Fudge Factory & General Store. There's a circus sideshow museum with more than a century's worth of artifacts on display and performers such as sword swallowers; a large candy and general store with all manner of souvenirs, most with slogans that use juvenile humor as a play on words about the site's name; miniature golf; a restaurant; and a towering neon sign with a dinosaur eating a flying saucer. This is Uranus.

Waynesville is another example of the old highway's unique nature in Missouri. The Roubidoux Creek Bridge built in 1923 and Laughlin Park along Roubidoux Creek are an urban oasis as well as a somber historic site.

This park was a campground on the Trail of Tears. Informative kiosks along the Trail of Tears Memorial and Interpretive Walking Trail tell the story of the Cherokee Nation during their forced relocation west to the Indian Territory between 1838 and 1839.

The historic heart of town is a blending of connections to Route 66 and to the town's long history. The Old Stagecoach Stop House Museum opened as the Waynesville House

BELOW, FROM TOP The earliest alignment of Route 66 is a narrow ribbon of asphalt that twists its way to a picturesque bridge that spans the Big Piney River.

Uranus with its garish neon signage, circus sideshow museum, escape rooms, juvenile humor displayed on all manner of souvenirs, and delicious fudge is a throwback to classic roadside attractions.

Built in 1923, this concrete arch bridge over the Roubidoux Creek frames one end of scenic and historic Laughlin Park on the edge of downtown Waynesville.

in about 1854. The Pulaski County Courthouse, built in 1903, is also a museum. It was here in 1990 that Governor John Ashcraft signed the bill designating Route 66 an historic highway in the state.

Lebanon is a modern, progressive community that is quite proud of its history and Route 66 association. The pièce de résistance of Route 66 destinations is the Munger Moss Motel that dates to 1946. This revered treasure with its 1950s-era neon signage attracts legions of international Route 66 enthusiasts.

In large part, this is due to the proprietor. Bob and Ramona Lehman purchased the property in 1971 and played an active role in the Route 66 renaissance. Ramona still manages the motel, and a recent anniversary celebration commemorating the Munger Moss Motel's seventy-fifth year

in Lebanon and the fiftieth year of ownership by Ramona and her late husband was attended by people from throughout the United States as well as Europe.

And then there are the unexpected surprises. In Marshfield, on the west side of the square, is a 1,200-pound (544.3 kg), one-quarter-scale replica of the Hubble Space Telescope. It is a monument to the town's favorite son, astronomer Edwin Powell Hubble who was born in Marshfield on November 20, 1889.

Springfield is a most interesting city with lots to see and do. However, as this city figures prominently in other drives, we will jump ahead to Paris Springs Junction and Spencer, two attractions of note. Both are located on an easily accessed older alignment of Route 66 that forms an "S" with the newer incarnation of that highway.

Paris Springs Junction, not to be confused with the long-vanished ghost town of Paris Springs located a short distance to the north, was never more than a wide spot in the road. To profit from the traffic along Route 66, a cobblestone garage was built at the junction. A service station, café, and some cabins were later added to the complex.

The owners, Fred and Gay Mason, named it Gay Parita. With realignment of the highway, only the garage and station were kept open. Gay died in 1953 and then the station burned down in 1955.

Fast-forward to the twenty-first century. As a retirement project, Gary and Lena Turner purchased the property, renovated the old garage, and built a replica Sinclair service station. With its vintage signage and gasoline pumps, old cars and trucks, and service station memorabilia, it appears as a tribute to

an earlier time. The Turners took it one step further with special touches such as inviting Route 66 travelers to sit, visit, and share cold watermelon. Gay Parita quickly became a destination for Route 66 travelers. Today, the Turner family continues that tradition.

Spencer is a very small community with decades of Missouri history. Its origins began with the establishment of Johnson's Mill built on Turnback Creek in about 1866. That creek is spanned by a 1923 steel-truss bridge, your portal to this earlier time.

By the late teens, the small village had become an almost complete ghost town. In 1925, after learning that U.S. 66 would be routed along the state highway, Sidney Casey purchased the town site including the old Spencer General Store.

He established a service station and garage. Another building was leased as a

LEFT Today Gay Parita has been transformed into a living time capsule that provides an opportunity to experience the Route 66 roadside of the early 1950s.

FAR LEFT The original stone garage served as the foundation for the modern incarnation at Gay Parita in Paris Springs Junction.

barbershop, and another become a café.
It proved to be a short-lived endeavor as
Route 66 was soon realigned to bypass the
narrow bridge on Turnback Creek.

Businesses closed, and the site was frozen
in time. Then, in about 2010, the Francis
Ryan family purchased the townsite and
refurbished business façades to appear as
they did in the 1930s. At any time, Spencer
is quite the photogenic location as it is, but
with a background of colorful forested fall
foliage, it becomes quite spectacular. Continuing west toward Carthage, the highway
passes through a bucolic, timeless world of
farms, wood lots, and faded little towns and
past boarded-up roadside businesses.

Built in 1895, the Jasper County Courthouse in Carthage, an architectural masterpiece, is the second most photographed
man-made site in the state. It dominates a
square lined with beautiful buildings built
in the late nineteenth century and early
twentieth century. Indicative of historic
integrity, the entire square, called the Carthage Courthouse Square Historic District,
was listed on the National Register of Historic Places in 1980.

A few blocks away is the renovated
Boots Court. Built in 1939 by Arthur Boots,
the motel is another peek into the past. As
part of the owner's vision to restore the
property to an authentic reproduction of a
hotel from 1949, there are no televisions.
Instead, the motel offers replicas of vintage
radios, the height of motel luxury at the
time, supporting their earlier slogan of a
"Radio in every room!"

JUNCTION 66 AND 71, CARTHAGE, MO.

Route 66 twists through the streets of Carterville and Webb City, old mining towns, before traversing Joplin and crossing the state line into Kansas. Each town is full of history and amply seasoned with associations to a time more than a century before.

The attractions in Joplin are diverse. At 215 West 34th Street, a few blocks from Route 66, stands a private garage and apartment complex. In 1933, Bonnie and Clyde engaged in a firefight with law enforcement from this apartment and before making their daring getaway, left Newton County Constable John Wesley Harryman and Joplin Police Detective Harry McGinnis dead in the driveway.

The Joplin History & Mineral Museum is a well-designed complex with an astounding array of exhibits. The entrance presents the illusion of entering a mine shaft. Exhibits range from personal effects that Bonnie and Clyde left behind when they fled Joplin to fossils and items related to Route 66 history.

Also located here is the National Historic Cookie Cutter Exhibit, The Joplin Sports Hall of Fame, and the Merle Evans & Circus Tent Miniature Circus Exhibit. Also part of the complex is The Everett J. Ritchie Tri-State Mineral Museum, featuring an array of mineral specimens that is considered one of the finest in the United States.

Traveling Route 66 in Missouri is an absolute delight. Enhance the adventure by considering the recommendation of the late Gary Turner at Gay Parita: "Take the time to sit and visit, linger over coffee at Shelly's in Cuba, make a detour to Red Oak II, and never look at your watch."

FROM LEFT Recently renovated with an eye for detail, the Boots Court masterfully blends modern amenities with a 1930s era atmosphere.

In Missouri, a drive along Route 66 that gently follows the contours of the Ozark Mountains feels like time travel.

DRIVE TWO
DISCOVER ST. LOUIS

EXPLORING ROUTE 66 IN ST. LOUIS is quite the challenge. In the course of the highway's history, it was realigned numerous times. Further complicating things is the fact that there were main, bypass, truck, and city routes. Now, factor in decades of highway construction that truncated alignments and some streets being transformed into one-way corridors.

To get the most from your odyssey in St. Louis, pick a place to hang your hat for a few days. That will serve as your base camp.

There is a diverse array of good hotels within sight of the city's famous Gateway Arch. But for something memorable, my recommendation is the Moonrise Hotel in the historic Delmar Loop district.

The hotel is a mere five-minute drive from Forest Park, site of the Saint Louis Art Museum, Saint Louis Zoo, and Missouri History Museum. As a bonus, the original alignment of Route 66 skirts the southern edges of the park.

Topped by a rotating moon complete with

ABOVE Mere minutes from the city's famous arch and the Mississippi River, the Delmar Loop District is amply seasoned with vintage gems.

craters, the hotel has a unique ambiance. The Twilight Room, an all-season rooftop bar, provides guests with breathtaking panoramic views of the city. The ever-changing colors of the lighted staircase and the iridescent walls in the lobby impart a refreshing sense of whimsy. Adding to this feeling are displays of vintage space toys, memorabilia from classic space movies, and even NASA exhibits.

Larger than Central Park in New York City, Forest Park opened June 24, 1876. Until completion of the Gateway Arch National Park, Forest Park was a focal point for showcasing the city. Several significant events took place here including the Louisiana Purchase Exposition, World's Fair of 1904, and the 1904 Summer Olympics.

Vestiges from these events remain to this day. The Saint Louis Art Museum and Missouri History Museum are housed in buildings constructed for the World's Fair.

The Laclede's Landing district on the Mississippi River, with the iconic Gateway Arch positioned prominently in the background, comprise the historic heart of the city. Legend has it that Pierre Laclède, a French explorer, established a trading post for the Louisiana Fur Company at this site in 1763. He chose a site near the confluence of the Missouri and Mississippi Rivers. Also influencing his decision was Fort de Chartres, a French fortification located on the opposite bank of the river.

This was once the center of the city's manufacturing, warehousing, and shipping district. Today, it is the city's vibrant center for dining and nightlife. This historic area, encompassing nine square blocks, is made up of refurbished nineteenth-century riverfront warehouses and commercial buildings converted into nightclubs, restaurants, and shops, making it a desirable destination for visitors and locals alike.

BELOW, FROM TOP The St. Louis Art Museum is housed in the Palace of Fine Arts building designed by Cass Gilbert for the 1904 Louisiana Purchase Exposition.

For more than a century Forest Park has been the city's cultural hub with the St. Louis Art Museum, Missouri History Museum, St. Louis Science Center, and other attractions.

The earliest alignment of Route 66 skirted Forest Park, an urban paradise that is larger than New York City's Central Park.

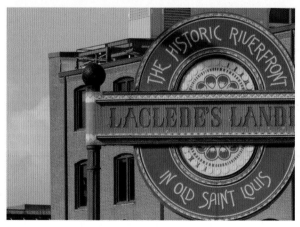

RIGHT, FROM TOP The opening of the Eads Bridge on July 4, 1874, was a gala celebration in St. Louis as well as East St. Louis.

Now a part of Gateway Arch National Park, the Old St. Louis County Courthouse built in 1828 served as a state and federal courthouse.

The Laclede's Landing district has been transformed from a gritty riverfront of 19th-century warehouses into a vibrant enclave of restaurants and nightclubs.

Located at Laclede's Landing is the Eads Bridge, a combination road and railway bridge over the Mississippi River connecting the city with East St. Louis, Illinois, that opened on July 4, 1874. At the time of construction, it was the world's first steel-truss bridge, and as the largest arch bridge ever built, it is considered an engineering marvel. As an historic sidenote, on opening day, to instill confidence in the construction of the bridge and to prove it was safe, John Robinson led a circus elephant across it to East St. Louis.

The bridge was named a National Historic Landmark by the National Park Service in 1964. Further recognition of its significance came in 1971 when it was named a National Historic Civil Engineering Landmark by the American Society of Civil Engineers.

The Gateway Arch, America's tallest monument, is at the center of a diverse array of attractions. I recommend that you start your visit by taking the Tram Ride to the Top to the observation gallery located an astounding 630 feet (192 m) above the city.

The Museum at the Gateway Arch interactive exhibits and displays chronicle more than two centuries of history. The story begins with the founding of St. Louis, follows the history of the 91-acre (36.8 ha) site and the role it played in American societal evolution, and culminates with construction of the Gateway Arch completed in 1965.

Framed by the arch is the Old Courthouse, a federal courthouse built in 1839 that is forever connected with a pivotal moment in American history. It was here in 1847 that Dred Scott, a slave, sued for his and his wife Harriet's freedom. The U.S. Supreme Court ruled that African Americans were not citizens and therefore they had no right to sue.

With tours offered since 1890, the North American headquarters of Anheuser-Busch is one of the oldest attractions in St. Louis. The brewery and buildings are world renowned for their architectural and artistic attributes and for the magnificent Budweiser Clydesdales.

West of the city in Kirkwood is the National Museum of Transportation established in 1944. Housed here is the largest collection of vehicles in the world including trains, locomotives, airplanes, cars, trucks, and horse-drawn vehicles. Did you know that at the dawning of the twentieth century there were several automobile manufacturers based in St. Louis?

Located a short distance off Route 66, the museum also has a connection to that storied highway. When the 1941 Coral Court Motel,

For more than a century, except for the Prohibition years, the Anheuser-Busch brewery and head-quarters has been a premier attraction in St. Louis.

an infamous Route 66 legend for decades, was demolished in 1995, materials were salvaged to build a complete and detailed bungalow for a display at the museum.

A portal to the golden age of Route 66 is Ted Drewes Frozen Custard at 6726 Chippewa. Ted Drewes Sr., a well-known tennis player in the 1920s, opened the roadside stand in 1941. Today, the business is still operated by the Drewes family and is cherished both by locals as well as Route 66 enthusiasts.

Just south of the city is Cliff Cave Park. Managed by St. Louis County Parks, this scenic park on the banks of the Mississippi River has miles of scenic trails. It is also an historic site of note. Known as "Indian Cave" by early explorers, in 1749, this property was deeded to John Baptiste D'Gamache in a Spanish Land Grant. In the closing years of the eighteenth century, French fur trappers established a tavern on the site and used the cave as a beer cellar. The rock walls at the park entrance date to 1868 when the Cliff Cave Wine Company purchased the property.

Contending with timetables and distance, few Route 66 travelers do more than give St. Louis a cursory visit. It deserves more than that—much more. This is a city with a rich and colorful history, dynamic neighborhoods and districts, and more than a few surprises.

Ted Drewes Sr., winner of the Muny Tennis Championships from 1925 to 1936, established this frozen custard stand in 1941.

DRIVE THREE
AN OZARK ADVENTURE

TO GET THE MOST FROM THIS FUN-filled drive, start by making reservations at the iconic Wagon Wheel Motel in Cuba for two nights. Fully renovated, the motel is the essence of the Route 66 experience made manifest. The stone cottages in a park-like setting and the friendliness of the proprietor impel the guest to simply rest under the towering trees and enjoy friendly conversation with other travelers.

Missouri Hick Bar-B-Que, located next door, is one of my recommendations for dinner, with superb barbecue and in the fall, locally brewed hard pumpkin cider. And as their website advises, "Make sure you all leave room for some cobbler." Another is Belmont Vineyards, located along Route 66 a few miles (5 to 6 km) to the west, which offers fine dining with a panoramic view of the Ozark hills. Then, to further enhance the sense of stepping back in time, enjoy a movie at the 19 Drive-In located on Highway 19.

This loop drive begins by heading west on Route 66, Highway ZZ. Points of interest that

ABOVE Missouri Hick with its rustic ambiance is an excellent place for dinner after a day of Route 66 adventures in the Ozark Mountains.

should not be overlooked include the Fanning 66 Outpost with its large selection of Ozark and Route 66 souvenirs, M Vineyards & Farms with fresh jams, locally produced honey, and slices of excellent pie for a picnic, and the Rosati Winery Museum.

In St. James, turn south on Highway 8, which merges with State Highway 68 a few miles (5 to 6 km) from town. Continue your scenic drive through the rolling farm country of the Ozark Mountains to the junction and continue east on Highway 8.

The first stop is delightful Maramec Spring Park. The tip of the day is to plan your visit for the months of fall, if possible. This is a spectacularly beautiful place at any time of the year, but with the addition of brightly colored foliage, you are assured the most amazing photos.

The discovery of rich iron ore deposits at the site in 1825 led to establishment of the Maramec Iron Works the following year. Easy access to an abundant hardwood forest that used to produce charcoal and numerous streams harnessed for waterpower provided the ideal location for the establishment and growth of a small company town that in 1876 had a population of nearly 500 people.

Remnants of the Iron Works framed by the forest are impressive. The Historic Drive loops through the forested hills and provides scenic views of the Meramec River Valley.

It also provides access to the Iron Works Cemetery and the old Open Pit Iron Mine.

But the main feature here is Maramec Spring, a natural wonder that is one of the largest freshwater springs in the state of Missouri. The water bubbles up from a depth of nearly 350 feet (106.7 m), the year-round average temperature is fifty-six degrees Fahrenheit (13.3°C), and the clarity is astounding. The paved path loops around the spring, allowing the visitor to see the wonder from different angles.

There are two museums in the park. The Maramec Museum centers on interactive displays about the Meramec River Valley. There are also interpretive programs taught by the park's naturalist. The Ozark Agricultural Museum provides visitors with an opportunity to experience life in the mountains during the late nineteenth and early twentieth centuries. In addition to displays of farm equipment and vehicles, there is a functioning blacksmith shop and broom-making exhibit. The Snack Shop, located next to the Ozark Agricultural Museum, sells traditional treats.

Other amenities in the park include a campground, picnic area, and miles of shady hiking trails. The Missouri Department of Conservation stocks Maramec Spring daily with rainbow trout. At The Company Store, a visitor can purchase a fishing license as well as fishing supplies.

BELOW Maramec Spring, with the ruins of the expansive historic iron works framed by thick forest, is one of Missouri's beauty spots.

FAR RIGHT The 4M Vineyards & Farms Grape Stand that hearkens to the roadside farm stores that were prolific along Route 66 in the 1950s is an ideal place for picnic supplies.

BELOW The quaint business district in Steelville is a wonderful blending of eclectic shops in 19th-century storefronts and historic diners.

BOTTOM Regional and traditional favorites have been quenching appetites of travelers and locals at Rich's Famous Burgers since 1955.

This drive continues along Highway 8 into the Meramec River Valley. As a popular paddle sport destination, it should be noted that there are several places along the highway that rent canoes and kayaks.

Located at the junction with Highway 19 is Steelville. This is largely a resort community for people rafting or canoeing area rivers and streams. But just a short distance from the cluster of modern gas stations, convenience stores, and strip malls is a diminutive historic business district that begs to be explored.

Aside from late-nineteenth-century storefronts that house an eclectic array of shops, there are some eateries of note. Rich's Famous Burgers has been "Stackin' em high since 1955." But delicious, made from scratch burgers are just one of the taste treats on the menu. My recommendation is the breakfast burger made with fresh local angus beef, bacon, and a sunny-side up egg on a toasted bun. As a side dish, go for the spicy fried pickles or fried green beans.

Less than a block away is the Spare Rib, a hole-in-the-wall diner that opened in 1929. Traditional, hearty meals are their specialty, all served with a smile and small-town friendliness.

The return to Cuba is on Highway 19. It is a short but scenic drive that brings you into town past the historic Rockfair Tavern, a classic roadhouse with a bar and restaurant built of locally quarried stone in 1934. This makes a great place to end a day of discovery on an Ozark adventure.

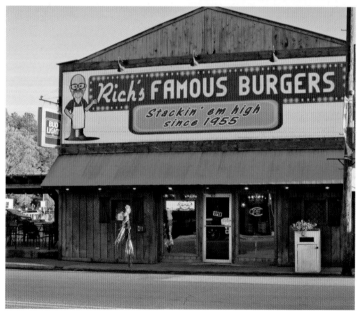

DRIVE FOUR
THE HEART OF THE OZARKS

THERE ARE THREE ROUTES FROM Springfield to Jefferson City, the state capital. Each is a journey through the stunning natural wonder of the Ozark Mountains. Each is amply peppered with attractions and charming villages. My personal favorite is U.S. 65, State Highway 73, and U.S. 54, a drive of about 150 miles (241.4 km).

The highway follows the twists and the foothills of the Ozark Mountains. The landscapes become ever more dramatic and beautiful as you draw closer to the Lake of the Ozarks. Just south of the lake is Ha Ha Tonka State Park, a delightful blending of scenic wonders, beautiful vistas, and photogenic historic sites.

Promoted as a "geologic wonderland featuring sinkholes, caves, a huge natural bridge, sheer bluffs, and Missouri's 12th largest spring," the park is a great place to stretch the legs. A highlight of a visit is the forested two-mile (3.2 km) loop trail to the imposing ruins of a stone castle situated on a bluff above the lake.

ABOVE The array of roadside businesses offering souvenirs, candies, and locally produced goods, as well as attractions, hints at the popularity of the Lake of the Ozarks as a destination.

In 1903, a wealthy investor from Kansas City, Robert M. Snyder, camping in the area found it so beautiful that he purchased large tracts of land. He planned on building a palatial retreat, and the original plans called for sixty rooms including a large dining area and salon with massive fireplace and panoramic windows. It was also to have a towering three-and-a-half story central atrium topped by a skylight and a landscaped garden.

Construction of locally quarried stone commenced in 1905. The project ended abruptly a few months later when Snyder was killed in an automobile accident. Years later, his sons resumed construction but not on as grand a scale as envisioned. It was completed in 1922, built overlooking a small lake.

With completion of the Bagnell Dam in 1931 and the creation of Lake of the Ozarks, the Snyder estate was divided by the rising waters. Capitalizing on the increase in area tourism fueled by the new lake, the castle was leased as a hotel until it burned in 1942.

The state of Missouri purchased the estate in 1978 and opened it to the public as the Ha Ha Tonka State Park. Today, it rates as one of the state's most popular parks.

It should be noted that Lake of the Ozarks is a resort area. Because of its popularity, there can be issues with traffic congestion.

The drive from Lake of the Ozarks to Jefferson City in the Missouri River Valley twists and turns through the wooded hills. It courses past old farms with barns and homes that hearken to the childhood years of President Harry Truman.

The beautiful state capitol building in Jefferson City, dedicated on October 6, 1924, is a real architectural feat. Built on a limestone bluff, the top of the dome towers more than 250 feet (76.2 m) above the city and casts long shadows on the Missouri River.

The capitol is more than the seat of state government. It is also a remarkable public

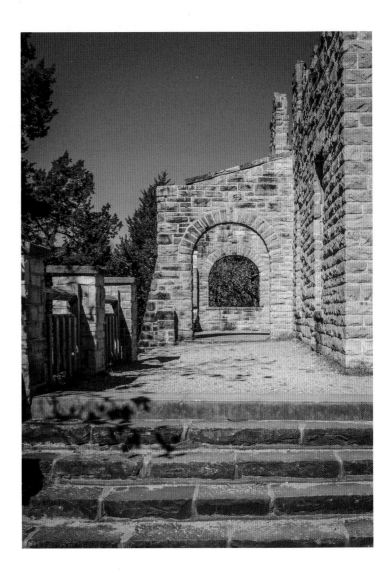

art museum. The centerpiece is the Thomas Hart Benton mural picturing *A Social History of the State of Missouri*, commissioned in 1935. Managed by the Missouri Department of Natural Resources, the Missouri State Museum, located on the ground floor, features an array of exhibits and dioramas chronicling the state's rich natural history as well as its evolution.

A forty-five-minute guided tour of the capitol is the best way to discover the building's secrets and unique architectural elements. A walk around the grounds dominated by sculptor Karl Bitter's bronze relief of the signing of the Louisiana Purchase Treaty is also

The scenic ruins of Robert M. Snyder's castle are a popular shade-dappled hiking and picnic destination in Ha Ha Tonka State Park.

recommended. For a wonderful photograph, I suggest capturing this sculpture at night and using the river as a backdrop.

The Museum of Missouri Military History is another attraction of interest in the city. Through exhibits, displays, and interactive kiosks, this museum chronicles the state's military history from the establishment of the Missouri Militia in 1808 to the modern era. Admission is free.

There are three options to tour the historic Missouri State Penitentiary: a paranormal tour, a history tour, and a photography tour. Dating to 1836, when it was decommissioned

LEFT The picturesque ruins of Robert M. Snyder's castle-like estate area are a popular attraction at Ha Ha Tonka State Park.

BELOW LEFT During the months of fall there is an entrancing beauty of a sunrise through the mist on the Lake of the Ozarks.

in 2004, this prison had the dubious distinction of being the oldest continually operated prison west of the Mississippi River. A stop at The Missouri State Penitentiary Museum rounds out the prison visit.

After exploring this dark, creepy, and fascinating place, you might want to consider an outing in the sunshine. Comprising old railroad beds, Katy Trail is ideal for nature lovers, bird-watchers, or people who enjoy a walk through the forest. Some sections are wheelchair accessible. And if you're ambitious, you can follow the trail until it connects with St. Charles and Clinton, Missouri, more than 220 miles (354.1 km)!

Jefferson City is a dynamic, vibrant, and historic city. As such, there is almost endless opportunity for unique dining experiences, like Prison Brews, a one-of-a-kind brew-pub housed in an old 1895 building on the east side. Add an excursion or two and this often-overlooked capital city becomes a very memorable Route 66 detour.

The Missouri state capital of Jefferson City on a hill above the Missouri River provides endless opportunity for capturing memorable photographs.

MINERS AND DESPERADOS

In honor and memory of these law enforcement officers who paid the supreme sacrifice while serving and protecting the citizens of Greene County.

The following six officers gave their lives Jan. 2, 1932 as they attempted to apprehend Jennings and Harry Young and their outlaw gang at a farm near Brookline, Missouri.

Marcell Hendrix
Sheriff 1887 – 1932

Wiley Mashburn
Deputy Sheriff 1883 – 1932

Charlie Houser
Springfield Police Department Patrol Driver 1903 – 1932

Sid Meadows
Police Detective 1885 – 1932

Ollie (Oliver Rufus) Crosswhite
Special Deputy 1889 – 1932

Tony Oliver
Chief of Detectives (Police Dept.) 1881 – 1932

Jerry Inman
Deputy Sheriff 1940 – 1968

Gary D. McCormack

John "Frank" Keller
1854 – 1895
Charles Kinser
1885 – 1925

THIS SHORT TRIP IS FOR ANYONE fascinated with true crime stories and obscure historic sites. And if you enjoy miles of beautiful scenery while driving the backroads, that is the bonus.

The adventure begins on Park Central Square in Springfield. It was here on July 21, 1865, that J. B. "Wild Bill" Hickok and Davis K. Tutt engaged in what is believed to the first Wild West shootout. The city's Public Works has developed a QR code–based tour with nine markers at the locations of witnesses that gave statements at the inquest. At each marker, a testimony is read by different narrators.

The next stop is Brookline, a small farming village that merged with the town of Republic in 2005. Both communities figure prominently in an incident known today as the Young Brothers Massacre.

While still in their teens, Paul and Jennings Young had developed a reputation in the Springfield area for theft, burglary, assorted crimes,

ABOVE This monument stands in mute testimony to a tragedy for local law enforcement agencies that was proclaimed in national headlines as the Young Brothers Massacre.

and violent tempers. Both were given short prison sentences for robbing a store near the family farm outside of Brookline.

After their release, the brothers, using the farm as a base of operations, built an interstate network for the sale of stolen merchandise. By 1929, they had added auto theft to their resume. Cars were stolen all along the Route 66 corridor from Amarillo, Texas, to Springfield, Illinois, and sold in Missouri, Arkansas, and Texas.

On June 2, 1929, Harry Young shot and killed City Marshall Mark Noe of Republic. Harry then fled to Texas.

On the afternoon of January 2, 1932, acting on a tip, the Springfield Chief of Police Ed Waddle, with Chief of Detectives Tony Oliver and several detectives, Sheriff Hendrix and two deputies, and a patrol officer initiated a raid on the farm. It was an epic gun battle.

It was also the largest single loss of law enforcement officers in a single incident before 9/11. A memorial to the officers stands at the Greene County Judicial Courts Facility in Springfield.

The next stop on this drive is outside Republic at Wilson's Creek National Battlefield established in 1960. The serenity of this bucolic and forested park is in stark contrast to the battle that raged here on August 10, 1861.

This was the first major Civil War battle fought west of the Mississippi River. Counted

among the casualties was General Nathaniel Lyon, the first Union general killed in action.

The Ray House has been renovated to its 1861 appearance. During the battle, this house served as a temporary field hospital for Confederate soldiers, and after his death on Bloody Hill, the body of General Nathaniel Lyon was laid on a bed in an upstairs bedroom.

A five-mile (8 km) road through the park is a self-guided tour with eight interpretive kiosks at significant locations associated with the battle. There are also five walking trails, each less than one mile (1.6 km) in length.

Continuing west on U.S. 60 through the Ozark Mountains foothills, the roadside is peppered with quaint farms. Small towns beckon the traveler to slow the speed and savor a cup of coffee with freshly baked apple pie at a little café.

Proclaimed to be the oldest mining town in southwest Missouri, Granby is a quaint village that deserves more than a cursory glance. The century-long mining history commenced in 1850 when Madison Vickery, a homesteader, discovered a rich deposit of galena, a lead ore, while digging along Gum Spring. The arrival of the railroad in 1856 and establishment of the Granby Mining & Smelting Company to smelt lead the following year marked the beginning of a mining industry that would flourish into the 1950s.

BELOW The visitor center at Wilson's Creek Battlefield, the trails, the drive, and the monuments add a somber feel to a beautiful, forested oasis.

BELOW, FAR LEFT In such a peaceful setting at Wilson's Creek Battlefield it is difficult to imagine the carnage and horrors of the battle that raged here on August 10, 1861.

LEFT The parks and greenspaces in Neosho give the town a pleasant and inviting feel that encourages the traveler to linger.

FAR LEFT Route 66 followed several different courses through Joplin and neighboring mining towns, but the city shows its pride in association with detailed signage.

Housed in an old mercantile, the oldest building on Main Street, the Miners Museum shares the exciting story of the town's mining history through photographs, mineral specimens, tools, and memorabilia. Two colorful murals on the outside wall portray area mining activities during the boom.

Neosho, Missouri, exemplifies the type of surprising discoveries to be made in these small villages. Did you know that it is here that you will find the nation's oldest operating federal fish hatchery established in 1888?

For good reason, Big Spring Park is proclaimed the crown jewel of Neosho. Renowned for its natural beauty, the most unique feature is the floral clock.

The original clock that cost the city $750 was shipped from Neuchâtel, Switzerland, and installed on June 15, 1967. Thousands of flowers and plants were used to fashion the seventeen-foot (5.2 m) clock face. It was a prominent attraction until its removal in 1995. In March 2020, a new clock and floral face were installed.

At 639 Young Street is a nondescript little building of tremendous historic significance.

Built in 1872, it served as the Neosho Colored School until 1891. This was the school that George Washington Carver attended during the 1876–77 school year.

In 1933, Clyde Barrow, using an alias, rented the garage and apartment complex located at 215 West 34th Street in Joplin as a hideout for his gang. For several weeks, they kept a low profile except for forays into neighboring communities like Neosho, where they robbed the Neosho Milling Company located on East Spring Street.

This drive wraps up in Joplin, a town proud of its Route 66 history. A great ending point is the Joplin History & Mineral Museum. Located in majestic Schifferdecker Park, the museum houses a collection of items recovered from the raid on Bonnie and Clyde's hideout.

The exhibit contains a camera and the photos developed by the *Joplin Globe*, including the infamous photo of Bonnie with pistol in her hand and cigar in her mouth pretending to hold Clyde at gunpoint.

Part Three
KANSAS

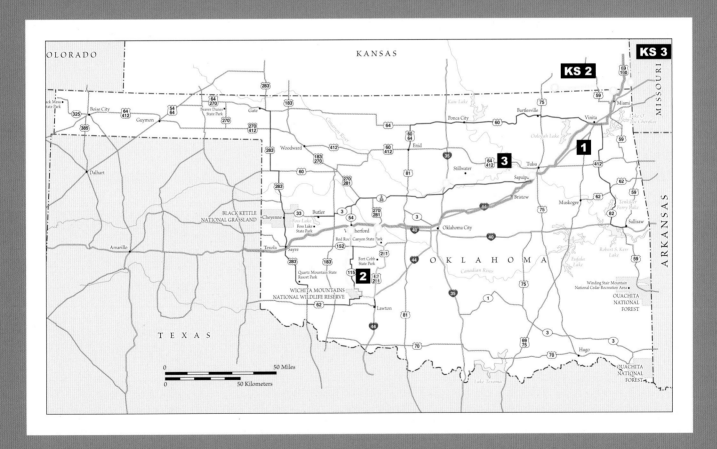

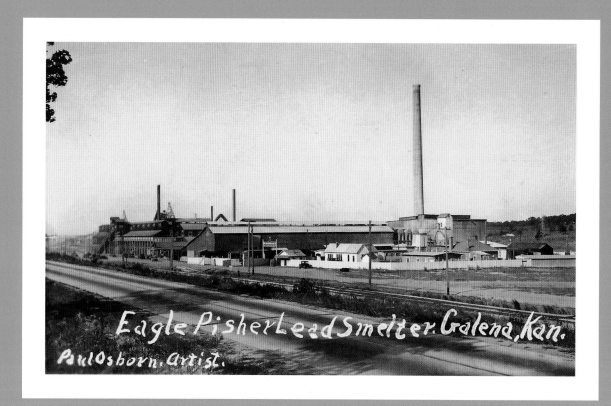

Eagle Picher Lead Smelter, Galena, Kan.
Paul Osborn, Artist.

ROUTE 66 CUTS THROUGH THE SOUTH-east corner of Kansas. From the Missouri to Oklahoma border, the drive is less than fifteen miles (24.1 km). But packed into each mile (1.6 km) is a staggering array of attractions including Civil War battlefields, museums, memorable Route 66 stops, and timeless diners that hearken to the golden days of Route 66.

West of Joplin, Missouri, four-lane Highway 66 provides the most direct access to Galena, Kansas. This was the latter "Bypass 66" alignment. I prefer to follow the road signed as Old 66 Boulevard

into Kansas and past the battered old State Line Bar & Grill.

Here, the road cuts through a gritty, long-abandoned industrial area before sweeping into Galena over an old viaduct. It was here at the site of the Eagle Picher Company, a smelter, that one of the most violent labor disputes of the 1930s took place.

John Lewis, president of the United Mine Workers, called a strike against this plant in 1935. The company responded by bringing in nonunion workers from neighboring communities

ABOVE One of the largest lead smelters in the country during the 1930s, the Eagle Picher Company became the focal point for a violent union strike that closed Route 66. **PREVIOUS, LEFT** After its destruction by a tornado in 1923, Leo Williams rebuilt in 1925 and enclosed the front portico in 1933 to accommodate a larger store.

in Missouri, Kansas, and Oklahoma. Angry mine workers responded by barricading Route 66, which forced sheriff's deputies to reroute traffic.

Escalation of the violence included fires, beatings, and sabotage. Governor Alf Landon, Republican presidential candidate in 1936, declared martial law, dispatched the National Guard to Galena, and forced the reopening of Route 66 with checkpoints.

Incorporated in 1877, Galena is the oldest mining town in Kansas. The name is from the lead ore mined through the early 1950s. In the years bracketing World War I, this corner of Kansas, the northeast corner of Oklahoma and the corner of southwestern Missouri, was the largest lead and zinc mining district in the world.

By the dawn of the twentieth century, Galena had morphed from a wild and wooly mining boomtown into a modern, progressive community. Between 1890 and 1900, the population grew more than 300 percent to over 10,000 people.

The decline of mining and smelting operations in the 1950s, and then the bypass of Route 66, decimated the town's economy. Still, it remains a small, vibrant village with people that are passionately proud of its history.

This is evident in the superb Galena Mining & Historical Museum, housed in the former Missouri, Kansas & Texas train depot. In addition to displays of historic artifacts and an expansive mineral collection, the museum also chronicles the city's ongoing revival fueled by the ever-growing international fascination with Route 66.

For the trivia buff, there is an interesting celebrity association with Galena. Harry Houdini made his debut as a "spiritualist" at a theater in this city on January 8, 1898.

Riverton is the next stop. The draw of note is the Eisler Brothers Old Riverton

BELOW In the years bracketing WW I, Galena was a boom-town at the heart of a tri-state lead and zinc mining district that was the largest in the world.

MIDDLE Colorful murals, renovated storefronts gaily lit with neon, and pleasant small parks give visitors to Galena a warm and inviting welcome.

BOTTOM The repurposed Missouri, Kansas & Texas train depot is home to the Galena Mining & Historical Museum with an expansive mineralogical display.

Store, now Nelson's Old Riverton Store. Established on March 20, 1925, to replace the store destroyed by a tornado, it thrived during the era of Route 66.

Apart from the shaded portico for the gas pumps that was transformed into a room with tables for deli customers, the store is virtually unchanged. This and the delicious gourmet sandwiches make this a very popular stop for legions of Route 66 enthusiasts.

Riverton is also the site of scenic Lowell Reservoir and the Empire District Electric Company. Established in 1909, this is one of the longest continuously operated power plants in the United States. Interestingly, one of the first generators the company acquired was "Old Kate," which had

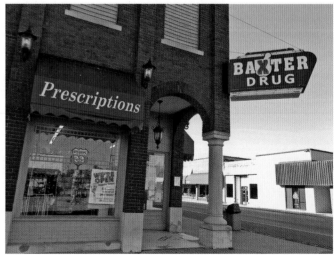

originally supplied power for the 1904 St. Louis World's Fair.

A short distance to the west on Beasley Road is Brush Creek Bridge. Listed on the National Register of Historic Places in 1983, this is one of the few remaining Marsh Arch bridges in the country. Designed and patented in 1912, the graceful concrete and steel design is unique. Built in 1923, it carried traffic between Galena and Baxter Springs until 1992. At that time, a new bridge was built to the east.

The refurbished bridge is a favored photo stop for Route 66 enthusiasts. In 2000, for The Learning Channel special program *Route 66: Main Street of America*, singer Brad Paisley performed the song "Route 66" on this bridge.

Nestled almost on the border with Oklahoma is Baxter Springs. Another faded mining town that exudes an infectious sense of vibrancy, Baxter Springs is full of surprises.

One example is the brick building on the corner at 1101 Military Avenue (Route 66). Built in 1876 as a community bank, it was purportedly robbed by the gang led by Jesse James and Cole Younger.

John Baxter built an inn and general store at the mineral springs along the military road in this corner of Kansas in about 1853. During the American Civil War, Fort Blaire, a military encampment for the Union Army, was established near the inn to protect the military road and other area assets.

An incident known today as the Baxter Springs Massacre occurred in 1863. After being repulsed during a savage attack on the encampment, a band of Confederate guerrillas known as Quantrill's Raiders surprised and decimated a military convoy led by Major General James Blunt.

The Baxter Springs Heritage Center and Museum at 8th Street and East Avenue should be the visitor's first stop. Here, you can pick up a map and brochure for a self-guided tour with twelve kiosks at key sites associated with the Battle at Baxter Springs and the Baxter Springs Massacre. This tour ends at the National Cemetery Plot with its memorial to those killed during those battles.

The twenty thousand square foot (1,858.1 m2) museum with an impressive array of professional displays is a very pleasant surprise. Chronicled here is the history of Baxter Springs from when the Osage Indians visited and camped at the springs they believed possessed healing powers through the present Route 66 era.

Baxter Springs was incorporated in 1868. Before the commencement of mining, the town boomed as a shipping point for Texas cattle on the Missouri River, Fort Scott & Gulf Railroad. This chapter of the town's story is also narrated at the museum.

As with Galena and Joplin, lead and zinc mining fueled rapid development that peaked shortly after World War I even though mining continued into the late 1950s. Buildings in the historic business district reflect this long and colorful history.

There is one more surprise from Baxter Springs to share. Legendary baseball player Mickey Mantle kicked off his professional career in Baxter Springs as a player with the minor league Baxter Springs Whiz Kids.

This drive on Route 66 in Kansas might be short on miles but it is long on smiles. Make sure to take the time to savor the adventure.

DRIVE TWO
GHOST TOWNS AND OUTLAWS

OUR DESTINATION ON THIS DRIVE IS Coffeyville, Kansas. It was here on October 5, 1892, that the notorious Dalton Gang met their demise in a now famous gun battle.

Except for a few valleys with rolling hills, U.S. 166 crosses the flat prairie past the scraps of old mining operations, shaded wood lots, and farms. And there are a few interesting villages to explore, some of which are on the fast track to becoming ghost towns.

Melrose still shows signs of life, but the best years are a distant memory. A post office

opened in 1877, but by 1905, the population had declined to such a point it closed. Still, the small population in town and the immediate area supports the Melrose United Methodist Church.

An Osage village was located at the site of Chetopa when a trading post was established here by Larkin McGhee in about 1847. Pioneers moved into the area in the early 1850s. Named for Chief Chetopa, the town was founded on April 18, 1857. A few years later, with tremendous fanfare, the Missouri, Kansas & Texas

ABOVE The raging gun battle that led to the death of members of the Dalton Gang transformed Coffeyville into a destination for those with a fascination for the macabre.

Railroad won the exclusive right to lay rails across the Indian Territories.

The Chetopa Historical Society established in 1946 manages the Chetopa Historical Museum. The museum houses eclectic but interesting displays of the town's long and intriguing history. Did you know that in the 1920s there was a factory that made buttons from mussel shells in Chetopa? Did you know that the town was once proclaimed "Pecan Capital of Kansas?"

Coffeyville was established along the Osage Black Dog Trail on the Verdigris River. Followed by hunting parties, the trail stretched from the mineral springs at Baxter Springs, Kansas, to the salt plains near the upper Arkansas River in Oklahoma.

It was named for Black Dog, a legendary Osage chief. A commanding figure, he was reportedly blind in his left eye, stood around seven feet tall (2.1 m), and weighed an estimated three hundred pounds (136.1 kg). His portrait was painted by George Catlin in 1834 and John Mix Stanley in 1843.

In about 1860, James Parker established a trading post on the east side of the river. A few years later, James A. Coffey established a trading post on the west side of the river. As homesteaders moved into the area, settlements developed along the river with the trading posts at the center.

In 1871, an iron bridge was built to span the Verdigris River at Parker, but Coffeyville, established in 1869, soon eclipsed its neighbor. Construction of the Missouri, Kansas & Texas Railroad and Leavenworth, Lawrence & Galveston Railroad fueled growth in Coffeyville and led to the abandonment of Parker.

Ranching and farming, and oil after 1881, ensured Coffeyville was a prosperous, vibrant community. On March 17, 1885, the First National Bank of Coffeyville was established. This and the Condon Bank were the targets of the Dalton Gang in 1892.

Before riding into Coffeyville that fateful October day, the Dalton Gang had honed a reputation by robbing trains throughout the Oklahoma territory. After riding into town, the men tied their horses to a fence in an alley close to the two banks.

Bob and Emmett Dalton were to rob the First National Bank. Grat Dalton, Dick Broadwell, and Bill Powers targeted the Condon Bank. But someone recognized the outlaws and quickly spread the word.

When the Dalton brothers walked out of the First National Bank, a fusillade of gunfire forced them to try to flee from the back door. There, too, they were met with a hail of bullets.

At the Condon Bank, a cashier delayed Grat Dalton, Powers, and Broadwell as he attempted to open the safe. As townspeople fired through the windows, the robbers grabbed loose cash and fled.

When the gun smoke cleared, except for Emmet Dalton, every member of the gang lay dead in the dirt. Four citizens had also been killed.

The story of the monumental gunfight is told through photographs and artifacts at the Dalton Defenders and Coffeyville History Museum located at 814 Walnut Street. The museum also houses an array of exhibits that chronicles the city's evolution.

A surprising display is of mementos associated with Wendell Willkie who lived and taught school in Coffeyville. Willkie was the 1940 Republican nominee for President of the United States. There is also an exhibit about Walter Johnson who lived in Coffeyville. Johnson was a pitcher for the Washington Senators. He was one of the first five players inducted into the Baseball Hall of Fame.

The diversity of attractions in Coffeyville is a pleasant surprise. The Aviation Heritage Museum, the Perkins Building, site of the Dalton raid, and the Midland Theater built in 1928 are just a few examples.

DRIVE THREE
THE PIONEER TRAIL

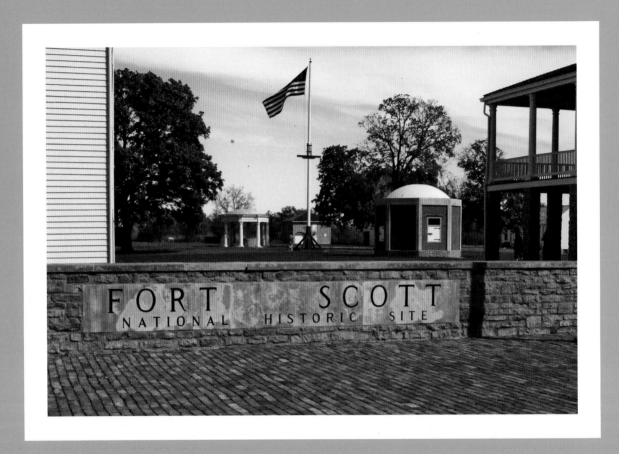

THIS IS ANOTHER SHORT ROUTE 66 side trip, just sixty miles (96.6 km) each way. Still, it exemplifies how much a short detour can enhance a Route 66 adventure.

The destination is Fort Scott, the preserved frontier-era military outpost and the fascinating town. Managed by the National Park Service, Fort Scott was established in 1842 on the Fort Leavenworth-Fort Gibson Military Road.

Named after General Winfield Scott, an acclaimed commander during the War of 1812 as well as the Mexican American War, Fort Scott played a pivotal role during several tumultuous periods on the western frontier.

With troops transferred to other outposts, the fort was abandoned in 1853. The empty outpost was the cornerstone for the town of Fort Scott, established on the site in 1855. During the Civil War, the fort was again commissioned and served as a major supply depot for Union forces and as a base for troops patrolling the military road. Confederate General Sterling

ABOVE With its original and recreated buildings, restored parade grounds, and its tallgrass prairie, Fort Scott is a frontier-era landmark.

Price stormed the fort twice but was unable to rout the garrison.

In 1862, troops were sent into the Indian Territory to protect the settlers. After the war, the fort and its garrison were to play an important role in the establishment of the first railroad line in southeast Kansas. The railroad and the town's location in a rich agricultural area ensured that Fort Scott grew as a prosperous, progressive community through the last decades of the nineteenth century.

In the late nineteenth century, the Molly Foster Berry Chapter of the Daughters of the American Revolution began a program that included the placement of commemorative plaques at sites associated with the town and fort's history. Shortly afterward, the Bourbon County Historical Society was established and, in partnership with the Business and Professional Women's Club, a museum was opened.

Surprisingly, in the 1950s, several buildings built during the Civil War still stood at the fort. These became the focal point for an initiative launched by Judge Harry Fisher. Joined by Kansas Congressman Joe Skubitz and Professor Dudley Cornish, Fisher was able to have Fort Scott designated a National Historic Landmark in 1964.

During this period, the city of Fort Scott established the Fort Scott Historical Park, a site that included the former parade grounds and numerous original buildings. In 1978, the city signed over the property for inclusion as a National Park.

ABOVE, CLOCKWISE FROM LEFT A visit to picturesque Fort Scott is almost like time travel to the years between the 1840s and 1870s on the western frontier.

Fort Scott was initially established to prevent infringement of treaties with Native Americans as settlers flooded into the area in the years before the Civil War.

From officers' quarters to the stockade and storerooms, attention to detail allows the visitor to step into the world of the mid-19th-century soldier on the western frontier.

Today, the park contains twenty historic structures, including nine that were reconstructed from original plans, on more than sixteen acres (6.5 ha). The buildings house thirty-three rooms furnished to reflect a mid-nineteenth-century military outpost. There are also five acres (2 ha) of restored tallgrass prairie that enhance the period feel.

The historic heart of the city of Fort Scott is an architectural wonderland. At the visitor information center, you can pick up a self-drive tour brochure to more than fifty stylish homes built between 1845 and 1919. The "Historic Downtown Fort Scott Walking Tour" is also highly recommended.

A unique and fascinating museum is the Lowell Milken Center for Unsung Heroes. It is an ongoing educational program and think tank that works with students and educators throughout the world. The goal is development of exhibits that highlight role models that had an impact on the course of history with exceptional displays of courage and compassion.

And after you work up an appetite from all the exploring, head to Penny's Diner. This classic 1950s-style American diner serves made fresh classics such as burgers and milk shakes.

For something a bit more upscale, there is Crooner's located in the historic downtown business district. They are acclaimed for their hand-cut steaks from locally grown beef and delicious poultry dishes.

If you're thirsty, there's the Boiler Room Brewhaus, Fort Scott's first microbrewery. The ambiance is as unique as the craft beer brewed on site as it is located in the old Downtowner building, a motel complex built in the 1950s.

Between Galena and Fort Scott is one more place of note, Pittsburgh. Established in 1876, for decades the town boomed as a zinc and coal mining town and as a center for railroad operations.

There are several museums in Pittsburgh and Crawford County that preserve this fascinating history. Each is unique.

A towering monument to mining in the area is Big Brutus at the Big Brutus Visitors Center located in West Mineral, Kansas, about twenty-three miles (37 km) southwest of Pittsburgh. Proclaimed to be one of the eight wonders of Kansas, Big Brutus is a Bucyrus-Erie model 1850-B electric shovel. During the 1960s and 1970s, this was the second largest electric shovel in the world. In 2018, Big Brutus was added to the National Register of Historic Places.

Long before arriving in West Mineral, you will see Big Brutus looming over the

The sign reads:

DOWNTOWN DIRECTORY

Sharky's Pub & Grub
"Good food & honest drink"
16 N. National Avenue

Treasure Hunt
Antiques & Collectibles
Primitives & Furniture
6 S. Main

Trader Dave's
Open every day 10am to 5pm
15 S. Scott Avenue
620.644.2947

Country Cupboard
Gifts & Collectables
Souvenirs & Decor
12 N. Main

Common Ground Coffee Co., Ltd.
116 S. Main Street
620.223.2499

La Hacienda
Authentic Mexican
Restaurant
22 S. Main

Lowell Milken Center
Historic Exhibits
4 S. Main Street 620.223.9991

Mayco Ace Hardware
"The Helpful Place"
205 Scott Ave

Holmtown Pub
Food & Cocktails
206 N. National

prairie. It stands 160 feet (48.8 m) tall, equal to a sixteen-story building. It weighs an astounding eleven million pounds (4,989,516 kg)! Visitors cannot climb to the top, but they can go as high as five stories to sit in the operator's seat and see the shovel's inner workings. The views of the countryside are well worth the climb. And you can pose for a one-of-a-kind photo standing inside the massive bucket.

The small museum located in the visitors center is quite interesting. Aside from chronicling the story of mining in the area, there are displays of mineral samples.

Chicken Annie's Original is a regional legend. This delightful restaurant dates to 1934.

That was the year that Ann Pichler began cooking dinner for miners after her husband was injured in a mining accident.

As the reputation for delicious chicken dinners grew, the parlor was transformed into a restaurant on Saturday evenings to accommodate diners. Then, the family added rooms and still were unable to meet demand. But customers were not deterred by the crowds, they simply ordered their meal and waited outside for their name to be called.

Annie retired in 1963, and Louella and Carl, her children, and their family, continued the tradition. In 1972, the current restaurant opened but the tradition for good food continues to this day.

Part Four

OKLAHOMA

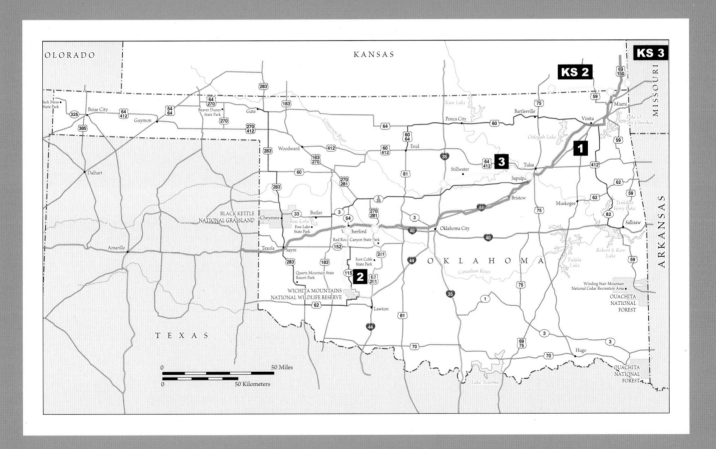

IF THE DRIVE ON ROUTE 66 IN OKLAHOMA was to have a central theme, it would be time travel. Small farming towns with cafés that opened before World War II, scenic bridges, forlorn ghost towns, and a highway that flows over rolling hills and into the prairie give this drive a sense of timelessness.

The iconic highway also cuts through two dynamic cities: Oklahoma City and Tulsa. Both cities are proud of their Route 66 connection; both cities are modern and progressive; and they are both firmly rooted in their history.

The drive begins with landscapes scarred by mining and the old mining towns of Quapaw, Commerce, and Miami. Each of these towns is worthy a bit of exploration.

On March 24, 1933, chief Victor Griffin of the Quapaw tribe laid a commemorative tablet made of locally mined zinc in the middle of Quapaw's Main Street. This was to celebrate completion of Highway 66 paving between Commerce, Oklahoma, and Baxter Springs, Kansas.

ABOVE The words of John Steinbeck in *The Grapes of Wrath* are brought to life with a drive along Route 66 in Oklahoma. **PREVIOUS, LEFT** Dating to the 1920s, Lucille's, with an apartment for the owner or manager above, is a rare example of an architectural style once common for rural service stations.

In Commerce, the Route 66 corridor is signed as Mickey Mantle Boulevard, an honorarium for the town's favorite son. His boyhood home, a private residence, is located at 310 South Quincy Street.

The town also has a Bonnie and Clyde connection. A small memorial dedicated to Constable William "Cal" Campbell killed by the gangster duo contains information about the shooting that occurred on April 6, 1934.

Counted among the assets in Miami is the beautiful Coleman Theatre built in 1929 at an astounding cost of $590,000. The city is also home to Waylan's Ku Ku, the last operating restaurant with original signage of a regional chain established in the mid-1960s. My tip is to try the delicious buffalo burger.

The earliest alignment of Route 66 between Miami and Narcissa is a true highway engineering oddity. The "Sidewalk Road" segment of highway was built as a state highway in 1922. Incredibly, the roadbed is only nine feet (2.7 m) wide with concrete edging!

Named for Lavinia Ellen "Vinnie" Ream, the sculptress that created the statue of Abraham Lincoln in the rotunda of the capital in Washington, D.C., Vinita is a charming farming town with a special prize. Owned by the same family since opening in 1927, Clanton's Cafe still serves superb chicken-fried steak and fresh berry cobbler.

The original alignment of Route 66 is signed as Andy Payne Boulevard in diminutive Foyil, Oklahoma. Andy Payne was the teenage Cherokee boy who won the Transcontinental Foot Race, known as the Bunion Derby, in 1928. A few miles (5 to 6 km) south of town is Ed Galloway's Totem Pole Park, a folk-art wonderland and picnic ground with

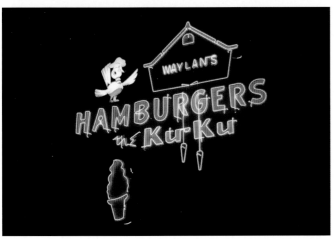

"The World's Largest Totem Pole" that dates to the 1930s.

There are two fascinating attractions in Claremore that should be added to a travel itinerary. One is the Will Rogers Memorial Museum that houses the entire collection of Will Rogers' writings and an array of exhibits displaying memorabilia such as movie posters and photographs.

The second attraction of note is the J. M. Davis Arms & Historical Museum. In addition to the world's largest collection of firearms manufactured from the fourteenth century to the modern era, there is a fascinating array of diverse displays. These include World War I and World War II recruitment posters from several countries, nineteenth-century music boxes, and Native American artifacts as well as guns and personal possessions belonging to infamous characters such as John Dillinger and Jesse James.

With the advent of the Interstate Highway System, quirky roadside attractions closed. In Catoosa, a rare survivor still welcomes Route 66 travelers. Recently refurbished, the famed Blue Whale, built between 1970 and 1972, with its surrounding picnic grounds, park, and pond, is a connection to vanished roadside Americana.

Tulsa is a dynamic, modern city. And in recent years, the city has become a leader in the development of innovative programs to

MASON HOTEL COFFEE SHOP, CLAREMORE, OKLAHOMA

J. M. DAVIS GUN COLLECTION, LARGEST INDIVIDUAL GUN COLLECTION IN U. S. A.

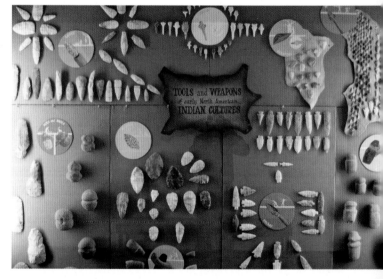

WILL ROGERS MEMORIAL CLAREMORE, OKLA.

revitalize the Route 66 corridor. Neon sign initiatives are restoring a colorful glow to the highway, and businesses such as the long-shuttered Campbell Hotel have been refurbished.

The first major project to be completed within the Vision 2025 Route 66 Enhancements and Promotion Master Plan of Development was phase one of Cyrus Avery Centennial Plaza on the Arkansas River. The centerpiece of the plaza is the incredibly detailed *East Meets West* sculpture created by Texas artist Robert Summers. It portrays Cyrus Avery, the proclaimed father of Route 66, and his family in a Model T encountering a horse-drawn freight wagon headed to town from the west Tulsa oil fields.

The Blue Dome District on the early alignment of Route 66 is a focal point for events such as the Blue Dome Arts Festival and Eat Street Tulsa food truck festival. It is also the heart of one of the city's most vibrant entertainment districts. Located at 2nd & Elgin, the district is named for the uniquely styled Blue Dome service station built in 1924.

Between Tulsa and Oklahoma City, the Route 66 corridor is amply seasoned with all manner of attractions, sites, old-school diners, and unexpected surprises. As an example, frozen in time on a hill above the highway is Depew. The original alignment of Route 66 passed down the main street but resultant of realignment, this village has the dubious distinction of being the first Route 66 community to be bypassed.

The renovated Rock Cafe has served locals and travelers alike in Stroud since summer 1939. Chandler is home to the wonderful Boomerang Diner, the 1939 Lincoln Motel, and the Chandler Route 66 Interpretive Center housed in The Chandler Armory built in 1937.

THE BLUE DOME, "BEST IN WEST", 2ND AND ELGIN, TULSA, OKLA.   104114

ABOVE, FROM TOP After years of neglect, the iconic Blue Whale and park have been refurbished and once again welcome Route 66 travelers.

Created by artist Robert Summers, the *East Meets West* sculpture captures the dramatic collision of past and future that was represented by the creation of U.S. 66.

The Blue Dome station was the first full-service station in Oklahoma to offer a car wash, Superoil products from the Chastain Oil Company, and free air for tires.

Chandler is also the location of Jerry McClanahan's gallery, McJerry's Route 66 Gallery. McClanahan, the author of the bestselling *EZ 66 Guide for Travelers* with hand-drawn maps, notes, and trivia, is an internationally acclaimed artist. The gallery is considered a destination for Route 66 enthusiasts who stop to view his work and to get an autograph in their guidebook.

Warwick is a ghost town. It is also home to Seaba Station, an artistically designed brick garage built in 1921. Today, it houses the Seaba Station Motorcycle Museum.

Arcadia has two well-known Route 66 attractions: one attraction links to the territorial era and one is an intriguing blend of 1950s malt shop and futuristic minimart.

The Arcadia Round Barn built in 1898 is today used as an event center, a visitor center, and it houses the Arcadia Historical and Preservation Society.

With a sixty-six-foot (20.1 m) illuminated soda pop bottle, complete with straw, out front along the highway, it is hard to overlook Pops. Nestled in the futuristically designed building is a gas station, a restaurant that mimics a 1950s diner, and a towering glass wall where sunlight filters through hundreds of different kinds of soda pop. Unsurprisingly, it is the soda pop that is Pops' claim to fame. Every brand and flavor imaginable are on display. Some leave you wondering who would buy them. Bacon-flavored soda pop?

As was the case in most metropolitan areas along the highway corridor, the course of Route 66 in Oklahoma City changed often. One alignment coursed around the state capital with functional oil derricks on the grounds.

There are so many attractions and sites to see that it would be easy to spend an entire week or two in the city. Many of these are found along the Route 66 corridors or within a short distance.

Frontier City, a pioneering amusement park that opened in 1958, is located along the post-1954 alignment of Route 66. The somber Oklahoma City National Memorial, commemorating the 1995 bombing of the Alfred P. Murrah Federal Building, is a few blocks from the alignment that ran through the middle of the city.

The National Cowboy and Western Heritage Museum at North 63D is a must-see attraction. The excitement of the western frontier and its heritage is brought to life through

LEFT Popular photo ops for Route 66 enthusiasts are ghost signs such as these on an old hotel in Chandler near the Boomerang Diner.

one of the world's foremost collections of classic and contemporary Western American art. This includes examples of work by masters such as Frederic Remington, Charles M. Russell, and sculptor James Earle Fraser.

Also on display are historic artifacts including firearms, rodeo memorabilia, and extensive displays on Native American culture.

Immediately west of the city in Bethany, the renovated Lake Overholser Bridge that originally opened in 1925 is of particular interest. Driving across the bridge provides

that sense of timelessness that is an integral part of the Route 66 experience. And when seen reflected in the lake at sunset or sunrise from beautiful Route 66 Park, you understand how important these historic bridges are for preservation of the highway's idiosyncratic nature.

Yukon, Oklahoma, is a town that has a distinctly western feel. That is enhanced by attractions such as the colorful Chisolm Trail mural, Yukon's Best Railroad Museum, and Garth Brooks Boulevard. But this is

ABOVE LEFT The 784-foot (239 m) reach of the Lake Overholser Bridge spanning the Canadian River was officially opened with great ceremony in August 1925.

ABOVE RIGHT Manifestations of Yukon's colorful western history such as murals, monuments, museums, and historic markers give the town a unique vibrancy.

Route 66, and that means communities are full of surprises. Since 1966, on the first weekend in October, Yukon celebrates its Czech heritage with the Oklahoma Czech Festival. This is the largest Czech cultural festival in the world outside the Czech Republic.

Historic Fort Reno is just west of El Reno along Route 66. Named for Major General Jesse Reno, the fort was established in 1875 to address the Cheyenne uprising. Today, the Fort Reno Visitor Center and Museum, and numerous historic buildings, house exhibits chronicling the rich history of the site that was used by the military for various purposes into the late 1940s.

An interesting site is the Fort Reno Post Cemetery. Aside from markers dating to the late nineteenth century on a hill with a sweeping view of the valley below, there is an official German and Italian military cemetery at the fort. These graves are the final resting place for World War II POWs.

The section of Route 66 between Fort Reno and Weatherford is a tangible link to the migration of the Okies, the Dust Bowl, and the Great Depression, even where it runs parallel to I-40. The 1933 pony truss bridge over the South Canadian River, the narrow roadbed with concrete curbing, and defunct businesses such as Lucille's Service Station that opened in the late 1920s, makes this drive seem like time travel.

Weatherford is a cornucopia of diverse attractions. Lucille's Roadhouse is a modern incarnation of the classic Route 66 diner. The food is superb. Named for astronaut Thomas P. Stafford, the Thomas P. Stafford Airport, Stafford Air & Space Museum, and Heartland of America Museum illustrate why Route 66 is often referenced as the crossroads of the past and future.

Clinton also has an array of diverse attractions. But the standout is the superb Oklahoma Route 66 Museum, one of the best on the route.

Elk City to the west has the Elk City Museum Complex. This includes the National Route 66 Museum, an interactive farm and ranch museum, and the Old Town Museum, an interesting museum dedicated to rodeo in western Oklahoma.

Except for Texola, the last towns on Route 66 in Oklahoma, Hext and Erick, are a bit too populated to be considered

LEFT, CLOCKWISE FROM TOP The Sandhills Curiosity Shop is a delightful and memorable blend of signs and Route 66 museum, curiosity shop, and bawdy vaudeville theatre.

In the ghost town of Texola, the old business district that dates to 1901 is being reclaimed by nature.

Tumbleweed Grill is more than a place to stop for pie and coffee, it is a glimpse of the future of Route 66 and a link to its past.

ghost towns, but there is ample evidence that these towns are mere shadows of what they once were. Surprisingly, there are some very interesting attractions that provide excellent subjects for some amazing photos.

In Erick, the two main streets, Sheb Wooley Avenue and Roger Miller Avenue, possess surprising celebrity association. These streets were named for two major celebrities that grew up in Erick. Then, there is the Sandhills Curiosity Shop, a bawdy vaudeville entertainment center and sign museum that cannot be explained. It must be experienced.

The business district in Texola that is being reclaimed by nature and the territorial-era jail make for haunting photos. But there is a faint hint of life in Texola.

The colorfully painted Tumbleweed Grill & Country Store stands in stark contrast to the rest of the faded old town. Inside is a hint of the 1930s. Old-fashioned burgers and similar dishes are the order of the day. But for me, I can't resist a stop for the apple pie and coffee. It seems the ideal way to wrap up a Route 66 adventure in Oklahoma.

DRIVE TWO
THE WESTERN FRONTIER

THIS FUN LITTLE SIDE TRIP, A DRIVE of less than eighty miles (128.7 km) along State Highway 33, is an opportunity to turn back the clock to the territorial era and the dawn of statehood. And as is often the case in Oklahoma, the countryside along the highway has a serene beauty, especially along the Cimarron River.

The adventure begins in Sapulpa, a delightful place that has managed to retain its identity and small-town charm even though it is on the fast track to becoming a suburb of Tulsa. In 1889, when the town was founded, this was District No. 8 in the Indian Territory.

The town thrived as it was at the center of an area of vast oil and natural gas reserves known as the Glenn Pool. In *A Guide Book to Highway 66* written by Jack Rittenhouse in 1946, he noted that, ". . . where fortunes were made in the early oil boom. One pair of investors started with $700 and ran their fortune up to $35 million in 11 years."

The opening of the Turner Turnpike in 1953 and the bypass of Route 66 decimated business for small motels and even restaurants. But one place of note survived and in the era of Route 66 renaissance is thriving, and that place is Happy Burger at 215 N. Mission Street. Originally opened as a Tastee Freez in 1957, it is the oldest restaurant still in operation in Sapulpa.

The first stop on this drive is historic Drumright. I suggest finding a place to park and exploring the historic heart of the small town as a walkabout. You might want to start with the Drumright Historical Museum housed in a beautiful 1915 Santa Fe depot. Listed on the National Register of Historic Places, the central lobby of the depot is adorned with large eight-foot (2.4 m) murals that chronicle the history of this part of central Oklahoma.

Told in richly detailed pictures is the history of Native Americans, their interaction with Spanish and French trappers and traders as well as American buffalo hunters, the Trail of Tears, and the discovery of oil.

As the town owes its existence to the discovery of the greatest oil field of the era on a farm in Creek County, the Oil Room in the museum is of particular interest. Outdoor exhibits include a collection of historic equipment used in the oil fields.

Shortly after the Drumright Field discovery in March 1912, more than eight thousand people swarmed into the area and almost overnight the towns of Drumright, Oilton, and Shamrock sprang from the prairie.

By 1917, the Cushing-Drumright Field was the largest oil producer in the world. The historic business district and surrounding neighborhoods reflect this time of tremendous prosperity with buildings and houses adorned with intricate architectural detail.

Joseph's Fine Foods is a decades-old staple of the community. Known for its superb steak and barbecue, the restaurant also has menu offerings that hint of the Syrian and Lebanese immigrants that played an important role in the area's development. This includes tabouli, cabbage rolls, and smoked brisket.

Cushing is rooted in the frontier era of Oklahoma. But it is also a modern, progressive community with an array of attractions.

The area was originally assigned as lands for the Sac and Fox Reservation. There was also an expanse of grazing land leased to the Turkey Track Ranch that had its headquarters located a few miles (5 to 6 km) north of present-day Cushing.

William "Billy Rae" Little, a government agent for the tribes, had selected a site in the Cimarron Valley for a townsite before joining the land rush of September 22, 1891. After the run, to establish his claim, Little built a homestead and then surveyed lots for his envisioned town.

On November 10, 1891, a post office was established, and the town was named for Marshall Cushing, private secretary to U.S. Postmaster General John Wanamaker. By 1900, the town was booming as a result of cotton and grain farms. There were cotton gins, grain elevators, hotels, a string of saloons along Main Street, blacksmith shops, numerous general stores, and three lumberyards.

On March 17, 1912, wildcatter Thomas B. Slick struck oil on a farm belonging to Frank M. Wheeler a few miles (5 to 6 km) east of town. It was reported that more than 250 wagons rolled into town within seven days.

This rich and exciting history is manifest in colorful murals and the architecture of the city's historic core. But if you really want a panoramic view of the village and central Oklahoma, consider paying a visit to the Oklahoma Skydiving Center. This is the state's largest skydiving school.

Food is a big part of a road trip adventure. Here, my recommendation is Naifeh's Deli and Grill. You are assured a wonderful and delicious meal at this local favorite that opened its doors in 1978. The burgers are excellent.

Guthrie, the destination for this drive, is an astute representation of the territorial era. Large portions of the downtown area constitute one of the largest historic districts on the National Register of Historic Places. There are more than two thousand buildings representing commercial architecture from the late nineteenth and early twentieth century.

Located thirty miles (48.3 km) north of Route 66 and Oklahoma City, Guthrie served as the state capital from 1907 to 1910. Its foundation is the proclamation signed by President Benjamin Harrison on April 22, 1889, that opened the "Unassigned Lands in Indian Territory" to non-Indian homesteaders. The event known as the Oklahoma Land Rush gave rise to the moniker Oklahoma "Sooners."

With a population of just over eleven thousand people, a few hundred fewer than at its peak in 1920, Guthrie has a pleasant small-town feel. There is also a vibrancy and

The historic heart of Cushing is a delightful blend of architectural styles and historic sites that are best discovered by walking through the old business district.

passionate pride in the town's history made manifest in preservation efforts and the eclectic array of superb restaurants.

And to enhance the visit, almost every weekend there is an event. First, there are the fun-filled annual events such as the '89er Day Celebration in April, the Guthrie Jazz Banjo Festival that takes place on Memorial Day weekend, and the wonderful Territorial Christmas celebration. Then, there are things such as the Guthrie Historic District trolley tour held each Saturday.

The city also hosts a surprising array of live theater and concert performances. There are also several interesting museums, each with a different story to tell. These include the Oklahoma Frontier Drug Store Museum, Oklahoma Territorial Museum and Carnegie Library, Owens Art Place Museum, and Oklahoma Territorial Capital Sports Museum.

Guthrie is a vibrant territorial-era city with eclectic shops and restaurants in late 19th century and early 20th century storefronts.

DRIVE THREE
DISCOVER TULSA

ESTABLISHMENT OF A MILITARY outpost at the confluence of the Grand, Verdigris, and Arkansas Rivers, and the relocation of Indian tribes from the southeast to this section of the Indian Territories in the 1820s, is the foundation for the establishment of Tulsa. According to Oklahoma historian George Shirk, the name Tulsa is derived from the word Tulsey, a Creek tribal community in Alabama.

The fledgling community that warranted a post office in March 1879 was uniquely diverse. Former slaves, Native Americans, European immigrants, Americans, and Mexicans all settled in Tulsa.

The discovery of oil at Red Fork four miles (6.4 km) to the west in 1901 transformed Tulsa into a boomtown. Proclaimed "The Oil Capitol of The World," the population soared from 7,298 people in 1907 to more than seventy thousand people in 1920.

The diversity and prosperity of the city was made manifest in the Greenwood District heralded as Black Wall Street. It was here in 1921

ABOVE The Blue Dome District is famous as an arts district with a vibrant nightlife, but also located here are classic diners, bars, and restaurants.

that the city's reputation for opportunity for diverse ethnic groups was shattered with a horrendous incident known as the Tulsa Race Massacre. Twenty-four hours after the violence erupted, thirty-five city blocks of the Greenwood District lay in smoldering ruins and at least three hundred people were dead.

The Greenwood Rising Museum that opened in the summer of 2021 is an excellent place to begin an adventure in Tulsa. I was unable to attend the opening but reports from friends gave the museum rave reviews. Harnessing the power of modern technologies such as projection mapping and holographic effects, the visitor can explore the dynamic and tragic history of the historic Greenwood District.

Route 66 primarily followed two different alignments in the city. Before 1932, it followed Admiral Place and 2nd Street. In 1933, the highway was rerouted along 11th and 10th Streets. Both corridors are an exciting blend of modern, progressive Tulsa and its association with Route 66. There is also ample evidence of the city's innovative initiatives to preserve landmarks and to restore a neon glow along the old highway.

The Cyrus Avery Centennial Plaza on the Arkansas River is a destination for legions of Route 66 enthusiasts. Some Route 66 attractions such as Buck Atom's Cosmic Curios with its towering twenty-one-foot (6.4 m) Buck Atom's Muffler Man are products of the Route 66 renaissance. Others such as the Desert Hills Motel with its beautiful vintage neon sign, the restored Meadow Gold sign, Talley's Café, and Arnold's Old Fashioned Hamburgers are classics.

Opened in 1925, the Blue Dome Station of the Chastain Oil Company was an instant phenomenon. Its unique styling with an apartment for the manager under the dome and innovative services such as Oklahoma's first car wash set it apart from competitors.

Today, it is the central point of the Blue Dome District, the city's premier nightlife district.

A national treasure is the Deco District where the city proudly enshrines the largest collection of art deco architecture in the country. The crown jewel is the luxurious Mayo Hotel that opened its doors in 1925 as a Tulsa showpiece. It has hosted sports legends such as Babe Ruth and presidents such as John F. Kennedy.

The Tulsa Arts District should also be included in a visit to Tulsa. Rich with galleries, museums, beautiful parks, and historic venues such as Cain's Ballroom, this district truly comes to life with events such as the First Friday Art Crawl. For more information about attractions and events in Tulsa, visit their website (https://visittulsa.com).

Restoration of the historic Meadow Gold sign and its installation on a commemorative kiosk was the catalyst for the Meadow Gold District revitalization.

DRIVE FOUR
DISCOVER SOONER STATE CAPITAL

OKLAHOMA CITY IS THE COUNTY SEAT of Oklahoma County and has been the state capital since June 11, 1910. The rugged frontier community was originally known as Oklahoma Station. The post office application was amended in December 1888 when the name was changed to Oklahoma. It was again amended on July 1, 1923, to Oklahoma City.

From 1926 until 1954, Route 66 followed Lincoln Avenue and 23rd Street around the state capital. A great place to start an Oklahoma City odyssey is the Oklahoma History Center located near the capitol building.

In late 2020, the Crossroads of Commerce exhibit opened at the Oklahoma History Center chronicling the evolution of the state's commercial and industrial development over the course of the past two centuries opened. One of the most dynamic exhibits, the ONEOK, Inc. Gallery, contains cultural and historical displays from the thirty-eight federally recognized American Indian tribes in Oklahoma.

ABOVE The only state capital that fronts Route 66 and the only state capital with operational oil derricks is in Oklahoma City.

The Harn Homestead in the shadow of the capital is a surprising discovery amid an urban setting. The Harn Homestead Museum is an outdoor complex where the visitor learns about life in territorial Oklahoma. The grounds surround a nineteenth-century Victorian-style home that has been furnished as it would have been in the territorial era.

The city's newest attraction is the First Americans Museum. The 175,000 square foot (16,258 m2) museum highlights First American history, culture, and art and hosts an array of educational programs. A unique aspect of the museum is Thirty Nine Restaurant, a restaurant that specializes in Native American–inspired cuisine and traditional foods. There is also a museum store, FAMstore, that sells handmade goods and arts produced by First American artists and craftspeople.

America's rich western history and culture are enshrined and preserved at The National Cowboy & Western Heritage Museum. Established in 1955, the museum also houses the world's largest collection of western art and sculpture including work by masters such as Frederic Remington and Charles M. Russell.

Other exhibits include Prosperity Junction, a detailed recreation of a late-nineteenth-century prairie town. Galleries profile Native American culture, the history of rodeos and cowboys, firearms, and western military history.

Oklahoma City is also home to some unique museums. The Museum of Osteology features hundreds of skeletons from the tiny hummingbird up to a massive forty-foot (12.2 m) humpback whale. There are displays on comparative anatomy as well as forensics and pathology.

Here, too, you will find the American Banjo Museum, the Museum of Woman Pilots, and Oklahoma City Ballet. But there is more to the city than historic sites and museums.

One example is the Bricktown District Water Taxi. For more than twenty years, locals as well as tourists have enjoyed the sights, sounds, and beauty of this district while floating down the Bricktown Canal. On a late summer's evening, this is truly a treat.

For something more ambitious and intoxicating, there are several bicycle tours. The Bikes & Brews Tour highlights the city's history and unique architecture as well as the city's celebrated craft beer breweries.

The Art & Architecture Tour Ride is a pleasant ride through some of the city's most vibrant districts and visits to key attractions. Throughout the journey, the guide shares stories about the city's history and architectural splendors.

And of course, there is an array of Route 66 sights that have become world famous such as the triangular Milk Bottle Grocery on Classen Street, the pre-1930 alignment of Route 66. Built in 1930, an eleven-foot (3.4 m)-tall metal milk bottle sign was added in 1948 to promote a local dairy.

Another draw is the renovated Tower Theatre that opened in 1937. Now a vibrant movie and live event center, the theater is the heart of the Uptown 23rd Street District. After many years of movie premieres and historic runs of classic films, the Tower Theatre closed in 1989. It was renovated and reopened in 2017.

As with Tulsa, it would be quite easy to fill a vacation or two in Oklahoma City. The best way to plan an Oklahoma City visit is to start with the city's tourism website (www.visitokc.com).

Built in the 1930s, the triangular "milk bottle building" is a landmark in Oklahoma City's Asian District along the original alignment of Route 66 on Classen Boulevard.

THE WILDERNESS

DESIGNATED A SCENIC ROUTE, THIS
drive begins with U.S. 281 and U.S. 62
south from Bridgeport to Lawton. It continues west on State Highway 49 through the
Wichita National Wildlife Refuge before turning
north on State Highway 54 to Weatherford.

The drive south is across the prairie and
through small towns where ranching and
farming are the mainstay as they have been for
more than a century. The small town of Binger

was the boyhood home of Major League Hall of
Fame inductee Johnny Bench.

Anadarko is a portal to the vibrant history and
culture of the First American people. A great place
to start is the Southern Plains Indian Museum.

Established in 1947, this museum tells the
story of the Kiowa, Comanche, Kiowa Apache,
Fort Sill Apache, Southern Cheyenne, Southern
Arapaho, Wichita, Caddo, and Delaware tribes.
Also highlighted is the work of modern Native

ABOVE Medicine Park evolved into a vacation destination for the rich, the famous, and the nefarious such as Will Rogers and Pretty Boy Floyd.

American artists. Anadarko is also home to the Wichita Tribal History Center and National Hall of Fame for Famous American Indians.

The vibrancy of the historic heart of the village is clearly evident. There is the one family–owned George's Department Store with its wonderful neon signage that has been in business since 1948. Another example is the U.S. Post Office & Kiowa Indian Agency building built in 1935. Listed on the National Historic Register of Historic Places, the lobby is a showpiece with a sixteen-panel mural that depicts the ceremonial and social life of the Plains Indians. The Treasury Department commissioned artist Stephen Mopope in 1936 to paint the mural. To complete the work, he was assisted by Spencer Asah and James Auchiah.

My recommendation is to explore the historic business district with a leisurely walk. And I also suggest lunch at the Soda Fountain Eatery in the Melton Drug building. Homemade desserts are their specialty. But this is after enjoying a hearty plate of chicken enchiladas, spicy chicken chili, or fresh soups.

The next stop of note is Lawton, home of historic Fort Sill established in 1869, one of the longest continuously operated military facilities in the country. Attractions abound in this colorful city.

Fort Sill National Historic Landmark & Museum is a treasure trove of artifacts from more than 150 years of Oklahoma military history. The complex consists of more than two dozen historic buildings. Here, you will also find the grave of Geronimo, the legendary Apache chief and warrior, with a towering memorial marker.

The U.S. Army Field Artillery Museum is also located at Fort Sill. Indoor and outdoor exhibits illustrate the evolution of weaponry from the Revolutionary War to the modern era.

Through an array of interactive exhibits, such as a replica of a territorial-era trading post, the story of settlement on the Oklahoma prairie is told at the Museum of the Great Plains. The Comanche National Museum & Cultural Center is another highly recommended stop.

This is also the gateway to the scenic wonders of the Wichita Mountain Wildlife Refuge since the visitor center is in Lawton. The 59,020-acre (23,884.6 ha) refuge is an oasis where time has stood still. Preserved here is a rare expanse of native mixed grass prairie. This diverse environment is a haven for native grazing species such as American bison, Rocky Mountain elk, and white-tailed deer as well as birds, reptiles, and amphibians. And as an historical legacy, Texas longhorn cattle also roam free.

Opportunities for outdoor recreation and picnicking abound in the Wildlife Refuge. There are miles of scenic trails for hiking and mountain biking, streams for fishing, and even rock-climbing classes. Depending on the time of year, there are nature and wildlife tours that depart from the visitor center.

Founded as a resort town in 1908, Medicine Park, with its historic jail and unique cobblestone constructed buildings, has risen from abandonment to become a popular destination.

Scenic drives provide access to many of the refuge's natural wonders. One of the most inspiring takes visitors to the summit of Mount Scott. The tallest of the Wichita Mountains is Mount Pinchot; at 2,476 feet (754.7 m), it is almost 1,300 feet (396.2 m) higher than the surrounding countryside.

Lodging in the refuge is limited to camping. At Doris Campground there are tent sites and RV sites with electric hookups, and at the Charon Garden Wilderness Area there is another campground for backpackers.

One of the most prominent features is the Forty-Foot Hole near Lost Lake where Cache Creek flows through a charming canyon in a series of waterfalls. Stretching for miles, the Parallel Forest is an unusual sight. Shortly after the dawn of the twentieth century, cedar trees were planted six feet (1.8 m) apart, but never harvested.

The drive north to Weatherford on Highway 54 is nearly one hundred miles (161 km) with few signs of civilization. It is a landscape of ranch land, rolling prairie hills, and small farms.

Weatherford is a vibrant modern community firmly rooted in the past. Agriculture as well as the oil and natural gas industries are its foundation.

The past from the mid-nineteenth century through the 1950s is preserved at the Heartland of America Museum established in the summer of 2007. With more than one hundred exhibits in a twelve thousand square foot (1,114.8 m2) building, a visit to the critically acclaimed museum can easily consume an afternoon.

Located along Route 66 is the Stafford Air & Space Museum. Named for Weatherford native Lt. General Thomas P. Stafford, a test pilot and astronaut, this is one of most comprehensive aeronautical museums in the Plains States.

There are more than 63,000 square feet (5,852.9 m2) of exhibits. In addition, there are outside exhibits including aircraft. Museum developers worked closely with NASA, the U.S. Air Force, and the Smithsonian Institution to amass their aerospace collection.

Part Five

TEXAS

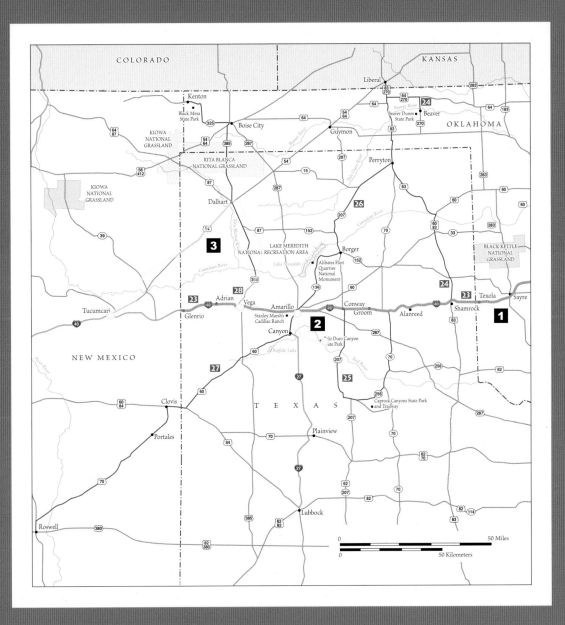

DRIVE ONE
ROUTE 66 IN THE TEXAS PANHANDLE

ROUTE 66 IN TEXAS BEGINS AND ENDS with ghost towns. On the east within spitting distance of the state line is Texola, Oklahoma. Straddling the New Mexico and Texas state line is Glenrio.

Aside from Kansas, Texas has the fewest number of miles in the eight-state Route 66 corridor, just over 175 miles (281.6 km). In between the border ghost towns are quaint small villages, dynamic Amarillo, and the rolling hills of the high plains that slowly give way to quintessential southwestern landscapes. And there are classic motels and diners and miles of open two-lane highway that hearken to Route 66 travel in the 1950s.

For westbound travelers on Route 66, Shamrock is the first stop in Texas. The town's origins make for an interesting story.

George Nickel (sometimes referenced as George Nichols), an Irish immigrant, filed the first application for a post office in 1890. But the post office never opened as the designated

ABOVE Aside from I-40 running parallel to the highway, the drive into Texas on Route 66 is just as it was in the 1950s. **PREVIOUS, LEFT** Dalhart is a warm and welcoming modern progressive community wrapped in what appears to be a rugged quintessential ranching town appearance.

building burned down. It was in 1902, the year that the Chicago, Rock Island & Gulf Railway reached the site, that the town was officially named Shamrock.

By 1911, the town was booming. There were two banks, a newspaper (*The Wheeler County Texan*), and a cotton mill. But surprisingly, water was hauled into town until a pipeline was completed from wells on the J.M. Porter Ranch in 1923.

The discovery of oil and certification of Route 66 in 1926 marked the beginning of a new era in Shamrock history. The city embraced Route 66 with a passion and in May 1932 hosted the U.S. Highway 66 Association convention.

The town still embraces its association with Route 66. Exemplifying this is the U-Drop Inn built in 1936. Now serving as the Shamrock Visitor Information Center, the renovated Art Deco masterpiece was immortalized as Radiator Springs, "Ramone's Body Shop" in the 2006 Pixar movie *Cars*.

The vintage Western Motel is located directly across the street. As a result, it has become a destination as Route 66 travelers enjoy the front-row seat when the neon trim and signage is lit on the U-Drop Inn at sunset.

Shamrock's progressive side is evident at the U-Drop Inn. There are state-of-the-art Tesla superchargers on site as well as charging facilities for other electric car brands. Its past is preserved at the Pioneer West Museum housed in the Reynolds Hotel that opened in 1928. The museum complex includes glimpses into the early period of Route 66, such as the renovated circa-1930 Magnolia Station.

It should come as no surprise to learn that the city's big event is the annual St. Patrick's Day Parade. But what might surprise you is this, the city has an actual piece of the legendary Blarney Stone. It is in Elmore Park.

BELOW, FROM TOP The iconic U-Drop Inn was built at the junction of U.S. 66 and U.S. 38 in 1936 by J.M. Tindall and R.C. Lewis. The U-Drop Inn with Tesla and EV charging stations illustrates how Route 66 is evolving in the era of renaissance. This renovated circa-1930 Magnolia service station at the Pioneer West Museum provides a glimpse of roadside America nearly a century ago.

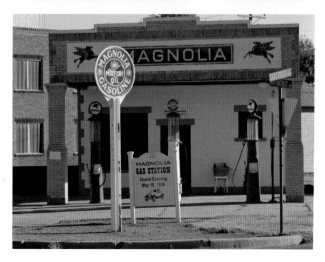

A group of residents with vision purchased the fragment in 1959 when it was offered for sale.

Much of Route 66 in Texas parallels I-40, which gives the illusion that the curtain separating past from present is quite thin. The exception is where it runs through communities like McLean, the last community on Route 66 in the state to be bypassed by the interstate.

McLean shows ample evidence that it could easily become a ghost town. But like rare flowers blooming in the desert, scattered about town are hints of a reawakening. One of these is the mid-1950s Cactus Inn Motel that is undergoing a full renovation. The Red River Steakhouse, opened in 1997, is another.

McLean was once home to a brassiere manufacturing company. That led to the town being unofficially known as "The Uplift Capital of the World." Today, that factory houses the intriguing Devil's Rope Museum and Route 66 Museum.

Perhaps the biggest surprise is discovering that a museum dedicated to the evolution and history of barbed wire is interesting. Another surprise is to learn that this dusty Panhandle town has a direct connection to the sinking of the Titanic.

Many of the towns along Route 66 in the Panhandle such as Lela, Alanreed, Jericho, and Conway were never much more than the proverbial wide spot in the road. Today, even that descriptor is no longer applicable. Still, many of these now-quiet places offer photographers a wonderful opportunity to capture the traces of what is left from the glory days of Route 66.

Jericho, however, has been given a new lease on life. And it now represents the future of Route 66 as we draw closer to the highway's centennial.

Before Route 66 was realigned in the early 1930s, Jericho, established in 1902,

CLOCKWISE FROM TOP LEFT As Route 66 serves as a business loop in some communities, and runs parallel to I-40 across the Panhandle, there is a blurring of the past and present.

Angela Moreland, who is renovating the mid-1950s Cactus Inn Motel, exemplifies the evolving nature of Route 66 as the highway's centennial draws near.

The former brassiere factory now houses the fascinating Devil's Rope and Old Route 66 Museum with an array of exhibits that chronicle the evolution of barbed wire.

thrived. There were three general stores, a tourist court, garage, service station, and other businesses. By 1955, the population no longer even warranted a post office, and it soon became a literal ghost town.

Blair and Blanca Schaffer, a young couple from Amarillo, recently purchased the town-site. Their ambitious plans include preservation stabilization of the old auto court, construction of a replica as well as an RV park with modern amenities, refurbishment of a farmhouse, and transforming the site into a Route 66 destination.

Groom, Texas, has faded since the bypass of Route 66, but it remains an active community with a motel, diner, and other businesses. Casting long shadows is the Cross of Our Lord Jesus Christ. Built in 1995, this 190-foot (59.7 m) monument and park with stations of the cross has become a popular destination for Route 66 travelers.

The unique nature of Amarillo is manifest in two of its most recognized Route 66 landmarks: the Cadillac Ranch and the Big Texan Steak Ranch. Ironically, neither of these sites is on Route 66!

In stark contrast is the Southwest 6th Avenue corridor, a section of the original alignment of Route 66 in the city. This is part of the San Jacinto Heights district platted in 1909. They aren't as recognizable, but here, too, are unusual links to Route 66 history.

To accommodate the increasing flow of traffic, Southwest 6th Avenue was widened twice: first in 1926 and again in 1942. As a result, numerous buildings, especially on the north side of the street, underwent extensive façade alterations that give these historic buildings a newer appearance than others in the neighborhood.

Today, this corridor is a delightful blend of nightclubs, restaurants, galleries, and antique stores. Counted among them is the GoldenLight Café opened in 1946.

ABOVE, FROM TOP At its peak in the 1930s, the farming town of Jericho had a business district with a general store, hardware store, tourist court, garage, and service station.

Route 66 in Groom is quiet today but The Grill, a diner, is still busy and the Chalet Inn still provides travelers with a restful night's sleep.

There are several alignments of Route 66 in Amarillo but surprisingly the city's most famous attractions for enthusiasts are not on that storied highway.

It was established by Chester "Pop" Ray, who was born in 1889, and his wife, Louise. He operated the café until 1957. A cantina was added in 1996 but the restaurant remains virtually unchanged. The hamburgers, buffalo burgers, and green chile burgers are still delicious.

All along the Route 66 corridors are tangible links to the city's association with that highway. There are also wonderful architectural finds such as the thirteen-story Santa Fe Railroad Building built between 1928 and 1930.

The drive west continues across the flat prairie, past vast feed lots and giant wind farms, and into Vega. Just a few blocks off Route 66 is a Magnolia Oil gas station refurbished to its original 1925 appearance.

The Milburn - Price Culture Museum should not be overlooked. Housed in a former general store with a colorful mural depicting the Comanchero traders, the diversity of the exhibits is a surprising find in such a small town. The area's agricultural and energy industry is chronicled; there is an operational nineteenth-century printing press; and an array of fascinating automobiles is on display.

Adrian, located a few miles (5 to 6 km) to the west, is world famous for the Midpoint

Cafe known for its delicious pies and the Midpoint sign marking the midpoint on Route 66 between Chicago and Santa Monica. The Midpoint Cafe is also connected to the history of Route 66. Opened in 1956 as Jesse's Café with a Dub's Enco Service Station next door, it is the oldest continuously operating Route 66 café between Amarillo, Texas, and Tucumcari, New Mexico.

Just west of Adrian, Route 66 is buried under I-40 almost all the way to the New Mexico line. This is where the landscape dramatically changes as it drops from the high plains down through hills of broken caprock and into a quintessential western landscape.

At Exit 0, you can drive south and reconnect with Route 66 in the ghost town of Glenrio. The empty four-lane highway with grass growing from the cracks and abandoned diner, motel, and gas stations stands in mute testimony to the era when Route 66 was literally the Main Street of America and the traffic flowed through Glenrio in an endless stream.

In 2007, the seventeen buildings in the business district from the period 1930 to the early 1960s and the highway roadbed were added to the National Register of Historic Places. One of the most popular sites is the Texas Longhorn Motel and Café. Dating to the early 1950s, the complex was once famous for its towering sign. One side read "Last Stop in Texas" while the other side read "First Stop in Texas."

A quirky part of the town's history resulted from Deaf Smith County, Texas, being dry. As the town sits astride the state line, businesses that sold alcohol were in New Mexico. The railroad depot, offices for the *Glenrio Tribune*, hardware store, Glenrio Hotel, and other businesses were in Texas.

The haunting and picturesque ruins in Glenrio make it one of the most photographed sites on Route 66 for enthusiasts.

DRIVE TWO
CANYONLANDS

AMARILLO SITS IN THIS MIDST OF A flat plain that stretches to the horizon in all directions. And yet, just thirty miles (48.3 km) to the south is a scenic wonderland of canyons and stone spires.

Head southwest from Amarillo on South Washington, which is County Road 1541. Continue to State Highway 217 and follow the signs to Palo Duro Canyon State Park. The focal point of the park is the eight hundred-foot (245.8 m)-deep "Grand Canyon of Texas" that is the second largest canyon in the United States.

Natural wonders are but a small part of the park's attraction. With archeological evidence that about twelve thousand years ago the Folsom and Clovis people called the canyons home, it is also an area rich in history.

More recently, the Apache, Comanche, and Kiowa lived in the Palo Duro area. Mesquite roots and beans, ample game, and other edibles

ABOVE One of the most famous rock formations in Palo Duro Canyon State Park is the Lighthouse that is accessed by a moderate three-mile (4.8 km) trail through the scenic wonderland.

provided sustenance. Petroglyphs, arrowheads, metates, and other relics are remnants from the pre-contact era. Remember, take nothing but photographs and leave nothing but footprints in the park.

Surprisingly, there is no historic record of Spanish exploration. Still, it is hard to imagine that they traveled across these prairies and never ventured into the literal oasis that is Palo Duro Canyon.

The canyon figures prominently in the Red River War, a series of battles between the U.S. Army and tribes of Southern Plains Indians. Between June 1874 and spring 1875, Colonel Ranald S. Mackenzie led the 4th U.S. Cavalry on numerous raids on Kiowa, Comanche, and Cheyenne encampments and ended Native American life in the canyons.

In 1876, Charles Goodnight, a pioneering rancher, drove more than 1,500 longhorn cattle to the canyon, and with John Adair, a British immigrant, founded the JA Ranch. At its height, the ranch grazed cattle on 1,325,000 acres (536,208.5 ha) in the Panhandle. The JA Ranch continues to operate today but on a much smaller scale.

In 1935, the state bought the land that constitutes Palo Duro Canyon State Park. The following year, a Civilian Conservation Corps camp was established in the park and workers built trails as well as cabins, a visitor center, and other buildings, many of which survive to this day.

Hiking trails provide access to some of the park's most outstanding sites. Trails range from moderate to difficult.

The stone cabins, three located on the canyon's rim and four on the canyon floor, remain a popular destination. They range from rustic without a bathroom to fully outfitted with air conditioning and small kitchen. Glamping, RV camping, and tent camping sites are also available. The park is close enough to Amarillo that you can easily make this a day trip.

The drive through Palo Duro Canyon State Park is in stark contrast to the featureless, almost drab landscape one expects to find in the Panhandle.

DRIVE THREE
TRAILS WEST

THIS DRIVE ALONG U.S. 385 AND U.S. 54 from Vega to Tucumcari, New Mexico, is less than 175 miles (281.6 km). And, it is the portal to the great southwest.

From Route 66, U.S. 385 flows north on Main Street in Vega past the Oldham County Courthouse built in 1915. The courthouse square, and the storefronts that surround it, seem suspended in time.

The drive north is through an arid landscape of twisted and weathered trees, empty prairie, and imposingly rugged hills that have a distinctly western feel. The highway crosses the Canadian River and passes through towns that are little more than names on a map.

This a vast landscape as exemplified by Channing, the Hartley County seat. As of 2019, the population was fewer than 275 people, and there were just thirty-eight businesses in town. Still, Channing is worth a cursory exploration, especially the uniquely styled Hartley County Courthouse that dates to 1906.

ABOVE Built in 1925 this Magnolia Oil gas station in Vega has been fully refurbished as a piece of history from roadside America at the infancy of Route 66.

As you draw closer to Dalhart, grain silos, farmhouses, and barns become numerous. But, some are long abandoned. This is a land of farmers and ranchers that for more than a century have battled the harsh environment.

Dalhart is a hardscrabble town with an infectious charm. Start with the courthouse square dominated by the Dallam County Courthouse built in 1923.

Nearby is the La Rita Performing Arts Theatre, another example of what makes Dalhart special. Construction on the theater commenced in the late 1920s, and it opened with great fanfare on February 4, 1931. A yellow brick façade topped with a woven patter of red bricks and the lovely marquis make this a star in the historic district that still retains red brick streets. The theater closed in about 1960 and remained dark for decades. In 1989, renovation commenced as it was transformed into the Dalhart Community Theater. In 1997, it officially became the La Rita Performing Arts Theatre, Inc.

This is another historic district that is best explored on foot. There are so many little gems and treasures awaiting discovery. And once you work up an appetite, there is the "10 in Texas," an authentic Texas steak house.

The New Mexico state line is a few miles (5 to 6 km) southwest of town on U.S. 54. And a few miles (5 to 6 km) past that is Nara Vista.

Just forty-nine miles (78.9 km) northeast of Tucumcari, this little town has a population that hovers around fifty people. But its history, classic sites, and the opportunity for remarkable photographs make this a town that begs to be explored.

Farms and ranches are rare outposts of civilization in the harsh and often barren-appearing Panhandle of west Texas.

The small village was first known as Narvaez. This was in deference to the Narvaez family that began ranching in the area about 1880.

The town's beginnings were not very auspicious. In 1901, Henry F. King, a railroad section foreman, converted a boxcar into a home for himself and his wife. He added a second boxcar to board railroad workers and itinerant cowboys.

In January 1902, a post office was established. Then, a railroad section house was built. Within a couple years, there was a school and a population large enough to support a couple of saloons, a general store, and a few other businesses.

The 1912–1913 edition of *Polk's Arizona and New Mexico Pictorial State Gazetteer and Business Directory* contained a lengthy list of businesses. These included the Manada Seed Company, several blacksmith shops, the Farmers & Merchants Trust & Savings Bank, First National Bank, a broom manufacturing enterprise, and a bakery. Also listed were saloons, a drug store, the Commercial Hotel and Hotel King, livery stables, a hardware store, a mortuary, a veterinarian, bakery, meat market, Herzstein, M. & Company general store, and restaurants.

There was also a newspaper, the short-lived *Nara Visa New Mexican*, which became the *Nara Visa New Mexican and Register* with Paul Jones as publisher after 1909. By 1920, Nara Visa, with a population of 651, was the second largest community in the county. Then, came the Great Depression and the Dust Bowl that sparked a downward spiral from which the town never recovered.

The Nara Vista School was built in 1921 and then closed in 1968 as there were only seven students. Today, the school and its auditorium are both listed on the National Register of Historic Places. It serves as a community center for the area.

Picturesque ruins and long-abandoned stores, restaurants, and bars along the highway hint at better times. But, they make it a photographer's paradise.

Just a few miles (5 to 6 km) from Tucumcari is Ute Lake Sate Park, a high desert oasis on the Canadian River. Almost thirteen miles (20.9 km) long, this is one of the longest lakes in the state. It is ideally suited for canoeing or kayaking. There are also miles of scenic hiking trails, campgrounds, and the Yucca RV Campground.

Ute Lake State Park on the Canadian River is a high desert on an oasis ideally suited for camping or a picnic.

Part Six
NEW MEXICO

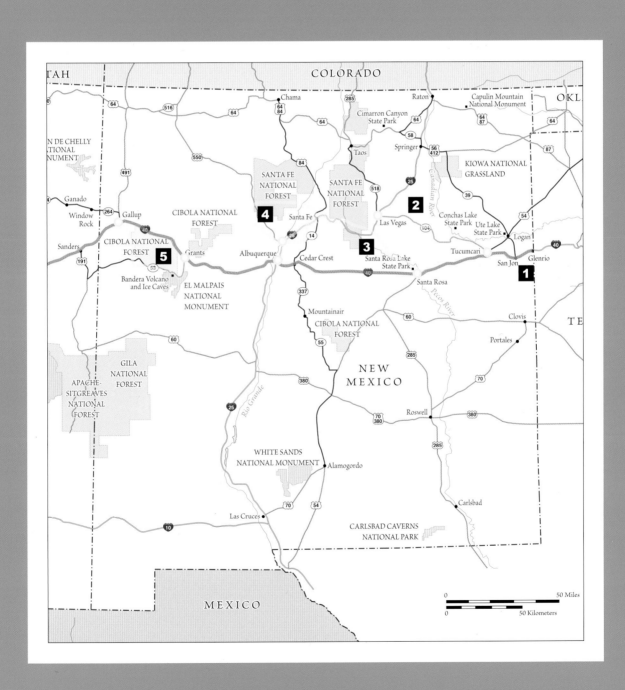

ROUTE 66 IN "THE LAND OF ENCHANTMENT"

ROUTE 66 HAS TWO DISTINCTLY different faces in New Mexico, "The Land of Enchantment." From the ghost town of Glenrio sitting astride the state line, the earliest alignment of Route 66, now a graded gravel road, rolls across the high desert, paralleling a long-abandoned railroad line and through the ghost town of Endee to San Jon.

The later alignment of the highway can be seen sweeping to the north where it is truncated by I-40. It is overgrown and gated to prevent access.

But if you follow I-40 into New Mexico, that deserted alignment can be accessed at the first exit and then followed through the forgotten town of Bard. And this provides an opportunity to visit Russell's Travel Center.

"Never judge a book by its cover" is an apt adage for this travel center. In addition to the restaurant, store, and amenities expected at a

ABOVE From the Texas state line the original alignment of Route 66, now a graded gravel road, flows across the high desert plain, through Endee and into San Jon. **PREVIOUS, LEFT** The three-story school built in 1903 is home to the Tucumcari Historical Museum with a diverse array of collections that chronicle the area's history.

modern truck stop, there is also a free Car and Collectible Museum with classic cars, ephemera from the ghost towns of Endee and Glenrio, and memorabilia from the heyday of Route 66.

From San Jon, Route 66 can be followed almost all the way into Tucumcari. Like many rural communities, Tucumcari was devastated by the bypass of Route 66, and there is ample evidence that it has yet to recover. There is also evidence that this is a town of passionate people proud of Tucumcari's frontier-era history and its association with Route 66 and with an eye on the future.

Scattered along the Route 66 corridor are neglected motels, stores, garages, and restaurants, but there are also renovated neon-lit sensations that act as time machines, transporting their visitors to an earlier age.

The Roadrunner Lodge has been refurbished with an eye for detail that allows the guest to experience a circa-1964 motel, but with modern amenities. The revered Blue Swallow Motel, with its colorful signage and renovated rooms, is a link to pre–World War II Route 66 travel. This is one of the most

ABOVE, TOP ROW The ghost town of Endee. It was here in 1906 that the last horse-mounted posse arrested cattle rustlers.

ABOVE, BELOW LEFT Forlorn relics and ever more impressive scenery are highlights of Route 66 from San Jon to Tucumcari..

ABOVE, BELOW RIGHT In Tucumcari the line between past and present is often blurred.

photographed properties on Route 66. Motel Safari dates to 1960 and is another icon that has been lovingly restored.

Tucumcari also has the modern Tucumcari Convention Center that houses a Route 66 Museum. But, this quaint town is more than just Route 66.

Mesalands Community College's Dinosaur Museum and Natural Sciences Laboratory is but one example of the diverse as well as fascinating attractions awaiting discovery. The museum offers annual paleontology field classes where participants take part in excavations in the rich fossil beds near town.

The ten thousand square foot (929 m2) exhibition hall houses a stunning array of fossils, original as well as replicas. One of the museum's most famous exhibits is the skeleton of a Torvosaurus, a forty-foot (12.2 m)-long relic from the Jurassic period. In addition to fossils, there is an expansive mineral and gem exhibit.

The city's rich railroad history is preserved at the Tucumcari Railroad Museum located in the renovated century-old Union Station depot. If you have the time, a visit to the Odeon Theater, built in 1936, has the ambiance to provide the perfect ending to a day spent exploring the history of Route 66.

Between Tucumcari and the Arizona state line, Route 66 is segmented and truncated. And yet, with the plethora of stunning landscapes, you are assured a memorable adventure with each mile driven on that storied highway.

Ghost towns, some with roots stretching to the era of Spanish colonization, and Native American villages that are even older, give Route 66 in New Mexico an exotic feel. Magnifying this are sites such as the Blue Hole in Santa Rosa.

The Blue Hole (Agua Negra Chiquita) on the original alignment of Route 66 was referenced as Blue Lake by early pioneers. It is

one of seven connected lakes and water-filled sink holes at Santa Rosa.

In 1932, the Blue Hole became a national fish hatchery. It transformed into the Blue Hole Recreation Area in the '70s and is now the Blue Hole Dive and Conference Center. As visibility is one hundred feet (30.5 m) or more, it has become a destination for scuba divers.

The beautiful twenty-five-acre (10.1 ha) Park Lake, with its stonework retaining walls, was built in the 1930s. It was, and is, a favored picnic place for Route 66 travelers.

From Santa Rosa there are two options. The first option is heading west directly to Albuquerque on the post-1937 alignment.

ABOVE, TOP The Route 66 corridor in Tucumcari is a string of memories, such as Roadrunner Lodge Motel, Teepee Curios, Blue Swallow Motel, and Kicks on 66.

ABOVE, BOTTOM Listed in the National Register of Historic Places, the Blue Swallow Motel that dates to 1939 is one of the most-photographed locations on Route 66.

The drive is largely on I-40 as that highway buried much of Route 66. Still, at the exits and along segments of the highway, such as between Moriarty and Albuquerque, there are some wonderful opportunities to cruise Route 66.

Clines Corners is a large modern travel plaza. But its origin began with a modest service station built at this highway junction by Ray Cline in 1934.

The Sunset Motel in Moriarty is the only remaining original Route 66 motel to still be owned by the same family since opening in the late 1950s. This motel has retained its nostalgic décor but offers its guests all the modern conveniences. The family takes tremendous pride in the property. From check-in to checkout, they proudly visit with guests, share family history, and show hidden parts of the property.

Before 1937, Route 66 looped from near Santa Rosa, through Santa Fe, and then south into Albuquerque. This alignment of the highway bridges the past, present, and more than one thousand years of history.

It begins by driving north on U.S. 84 from Exit 256 on I-40 a few miles (5 to 6 km) west of Santa Rosa to I-25. This highway is not Route 66, but in many places, it parallels the double six.

ABOVE LEFT, TOP AND BOTTOM The aptly named Blue Hole is one of seven lakes linked by an underwater flow that makes Santa Rosa a true desert oasis.

ABOVE RIGHT Pride in ownership is evident at the Sunset Motel in Moriarty, one of the oldest family-owned motels on Route 66.

Many portions of the original alignment of Route 66 that run along I-25 toward Santa Fe were once the National Old Trails Highway. And in some places, the iconic highway follows the historic Santa Fe Trail. Against a setting of pine-forested valleys, towering mountains, and deep canyons, the towns, villages, and ghost towns along the highway blur the line between past and present.

Tecolote has as its base the establishment of a farm by Salvador Montoya in 1824. Bernal was the site of the first stage stop east of Las Vegas on the Santa Fe Trail.

San Jose on the Pecos River can trace its origins to settlement in 1803. The little adobe chapel built sometime in the 1820s has cast a shadow on the Santa Fe Trail, National Old Trails Road, and Route 66. At the east end of town is an iron truss bridge over the Pecos River built in 1921.

There is historical reference of settlement at Pecos dated 1700. Nearby is Pecos National Historic Park where the sprawling, towering ruins of an ancient city are preserved.

In the late sixteenth century, the cartographer traveling with the Coronado expedition noted that this was the largest city encountered north of Mexico City. There is archeological evidence to indicate that people were living on this site along the Pecos River as early as 3500 BCE.

Satellite pueblos date to about 600 CE. The main site, the city itself, dates to the early fifteenth century. It developed as a major trading center for tribes throughout the Plains as well as those living in villages in present-day New Mexico. It is estimated that at its peak more than two thousand people resided here.

Aside from expansive pueblo ruins and breathtaking scenery, there are other historic sites of note. The thick adobe walls of Mission Nuestra Señora de los Ángeles de Porciúncula de los Pecos built in 1619 still tower above the valley.

Built to carry National Old Trails Road traffic across the Pecos River, this bridge built in 1921 is recent history in San Jose.

BACKROADS OF ROUTE 66

Close by is Kozlowski's Stage Stop and Trading Post, an important stop for travelers on the Santa Fe Trail, built in 1858. This would become the foundation for the expansive Forked Lightning Ranch. The ranch would later be owned by Colonel Elijah Edwin "Buddy" Fogelson and his wife Greer Garson.

To the west is Pigeon Ranch, a forlorn adobe structure preserved in an arrested state of decay that is another place of interest. Dating to the 1850s, this is the last remnant of a hostelry along the Santa Fe Trail. This building served as a hospital during the Battle of Glorieta Pass in March 1862. And during the era of the National Old Trails Road, and the infancy of Route 66, it was a tourist attraction.

Santa Fe is, as it was when Emily Post and Edsel Ford followed the National Old Trails Road into town during the summer of 1915, a truly one-of-a-kind city. Built on the ruins of a long-abandoned pueblo, Santa Fe was established in 1609.

Palpable links to centuries of history abound. The San Miguel Chapel built using the remains of a twelfth-century pueblo dates to 1610. Also built in 1610 was the Palace of the Governors. Now a museum, this is proclaimed to be the oldest European-built public building in continuous use within the continental United States.

A walking tour is the best way to explore the historic heart of the ancient city. Intermingled on twisted, narrow streets are homes, shops, and storefronts built over the course of several centuries.

As to lodging, the La Fonda on the Plaza, the only hotel built on the Santa Fe Plaza, was established in 1922. When completed, this hotel was a trophy in the Fred Harvey chain. But, according to history, a hotel has stood on this corner since at least 1612.

BELOW, FROM TOP Preserved at Pecos National Historic Park are the expansive ruins of a city that was at the heart of a vast trading network before the arrival of Spanish conquistadors.

The last vestiges of the Pigeon Ranch are a link to the Santa Fe Trail, American Civil War, National Old Trails Road, and Route 66.

For centuries travelers have been enamored by the vibrant diversity of Santa Fe where the flags of Spain, Mexico, the Confederate States of America, and the United States have flown.

OLD PIGEON RANCH ON SANTA FE TRAIL, NEW MEXICO.

AT THE END OF THE SANTA FE TRAIL TODAY, SANTA FE, NEW MEXICO

Another historic lodging option is the El Rey Court that opened in 1936. The renovated property is also an urban garden paradise with five acres (2 ha) of landscaped gardens that serves as a nationally recognized bird sanctuary.

From Santa Fe to Albuquerque, the old highway is intertwined with I-25. It is also entwined with portions of the Spanish colonial-era El Camino Real de Tierra Adentro.

In Albuquerque, the duality of Route 66 is again exposed. The early alignment runs north to south along 4th Street and toward the Isleta Pueblo. The latter alignment runs east to west along Central Avenue.

Both alignments are peppered with physical links to the city's association with Route 66. You will also discover links to the city's centuries of history.

Historic Old Town Albuquerque is a must-see destination. Nestled in the city's original core are more than 150 stores, restaurants, and galleries housed in historic buildings that date to the eighteenth and early nineteenth centuries.

The San Felipe de Neri Parish dominates the north side of the plaza in Old Town. Built in 1793, it is the oldest building in the city.

From Albuquerque to the Arizona state line, Route 66 is savored in snippets. I-40 has dissected it into segments.

ABOVE, TOP LEFT The El Rey Auto Court, now the El Rey Inn, opened in 1936 along Route 66 mere months before the highway was realigned to bypass Santa Fe.

ABOVE, BOTTOM LEFT Established in 1956 by Del Webb, the Hiway House Motel chain has vanished and only this example with its original signage remains.

ABOVE RIGHT AND OPPOSITE The Historic Old Town District with its swirl of galleries, restaurants, and shops in centuries-old storefronts seems out of place in a dynamic modern city.

However, connections to this storied highway abound. Take for example the Rio Puerco Bridge built in 1933 that is marooned between a frontage road and I-40 on a hill just above the Route 66 Casino.

One section of scenic Route 66 twists through Laguna Pueblo land. I would be remiss if it were not noted that there are strictly enforced regulations pertaining to photography. Still, a respectful visit to the village is highly recommended. It predates the arrival of the Spanish that built the San Jose Mission in 1699.

Another segment of Route 66 courses through the faded village of Cubero with its quaint adobe ruins. In the seventeenth century, Spanish cartographers noted a pueblo at the crossroads of a trade route at this site. A map created in 1776 indicates a small Spanish farming village had replaced the pueblo.

Before reaching the Arizona border, Route 66 passes by boarded-up cafés and trading posts and through the fascinating towns of Grants and Gallup. Each is framed by vast landscapes of towering buttes and mesas and desert plains that stretch toward the horizon.

The bypass of Route 66, and cessation of uranium mining, hit Grants hard and it shows. But this old town has seen lots of ups and downs since it was established as a railroad construction camp in 1881.

The New Mexico Mining Museum should be included in a Route 66 odyssey. The highlight is a self-guided tour through a simulated underground uranium mine. And be sure to grab a photo with the colorful neon Route 66 Drive-Thru Sign located on the grounds of the mining museum.

Gallup, located a few miles (5 to 6 km) from where the highway crosses into Arizona through a wide valley bordered by towering walls of stone, is a heady blending of Native American culture, frontier-era New Mexico,

BELOW, FROM TOP Bypassed with realignment of Route 66 in 1937, the faded old town of Cubero dates to the late 18th century.

As relics from the glory days of Route 66 are plentiful, even the dead end segments of Route 66 in scenic western New Mexico are well worth exploring.

The last of three theaters in Grants, the West Theatre built by owner C.E. Means opened in April 1959 and was refurbished with twin screens.

railroad history, and classic Route 66. This diversity is reflected in attractions, architecture, food, lodging options, and restaurants.

Earl's Family Restaurant dates to 1947. Aside from traditional American food, they offer New Mexican and regional specialties. And Native Americans sell their hand-crafted works on the shaded portico in front of the restaurant as they have for decades.

The one family–owned Richardson Trading Post opened in 1913. This is an authentic trading post that provides a valuable service to tribal members in the Gallup area. And its historic neon sign that has cast a glow on Route 66 for more than sixty years is a popular photo spot.

Built in 1937 and promoted as the "World's Largest Ranch House," the Hotel El Rancho is a real standout. As many movies were filmed in the area during the 1940s and 1950s, this hotel became a popular hangout for celebrities. The mezzanine is lined with autographed photos, and John Wayne kept a suite off the bar.

The dining room appears to be unchanged from the 1940s. Regional favorites such as atole, a blue corn mush called Tóshchíín in the Navajo language, adds an exotic touch.

Route 66 in New Mexico is a grand adventure. Drive the highway from border to border and you will see why this state is known as "The Land of Enchantment."

ABOVE, CLOCKWISE FROM LEFT The dining room at the El Rancho appears unchanged from when the resort hotel opened on December 17, 1937.

Native American association and culture has been an integral part of Gallup's identity and a focal point for tourism promotion since before the era of the National Old Trails Road.

Driving Route 66 through the Land of Enchantment is a journey through time that spans centuries of history and rich cultural diversity.

DRIVE TWO
THE ORIGINAL LAS VEGAS

IT IS A DRIVE OF JUST 110 MILES (177 KM) from Tucumcari to the original Las Vegas on State Highway 104. But an argument could easily be made that this is one of the most beautiful drives in the state. And Las Vegas is a town with a surprise on every street.

Initially, the drive is through quintessential high desert landscapes of dry arroyos, eroded hills, and desert plains with rugged mountains on the horizon. The highway twists and turns as it flows with the contours of the land and climbs toward the Canadian Escarpment.

Conchas Lake State Park on the Canadian River is a desert oasis. Miles of hiking trails course through the hills around one of the state's largest lakes. There are campsites and an RV park as well as visitor center with exhibits showcasing the areas wildlife and history.

Scattered here and there are old ranch houses and small villages such as Garita that dates to 1872. Uniquely designed abandoned old bridges are the remains of an older highway.

ABOVE The first stop on the highway 104 drive from Tucumcari to Las Vegas is a stop at the city's renovated 1924 depot that is now an interesting railroad museum.

As the highway climbs the steep Canadian Escarpment, the views become ever more majestic. Use the pullouts and savor the view.

From the summit of the Escarpment to Las Vegas, the landscape is noticeably different. At this elevation, it is mostly grass-covered gently rolling hills.

There is ample evidence that the broad valley of Nuestra Señora de los Dolores de Las Vegas Grandes has been occupied since at least 8,000 BCE. Pueblo Indians built complexes and even cities in the area between 1100 and 1500 CE.

Then, Comanche tribes hunted and camped in the valley before the arrival of Spanish explorers, beginning with Coronado in 1541. And by the closing years of the eighteenth century, Spanish farms, ranches, and settlements were spreading from the

Rio Grande Valley to the eastern face of the Sangre de Cristo Mountains.

Attesting to the unique nature of Las Vegas is the fact that there are more than nine hundred buildings listed on the National Register of Historic Places. And this is in a town with a population of fewer than 14,000 people!

Even more intriguing is this: until the late 1960s, this was two towns. The original or Old Las Vegas developed along the Santa Fe Trail. It was established in about 1835. The new town developed along the railroad after 1879.

The centerpiece of the Railroad Avenue Historic District, about one mile (1.6 km) east of Old Town Las Vegas, is the Castaneda. This lovely hotel that opened in 1898 was the pride of the Fred Harvey chain. Teddy Roosevelt hosted a reunion for the

Time seems to have been suspended in Las Vegas where the Santa Fe Trail courses through the business district and storefronts on the plaza date back to the 1840s.

Rough Riders at this hotel. After more than a half century of closure, the property was fully renovated with an attention to preservation and reopened in 2019.

Nearby is the El Fidel Hotel that opened for business on June 7, 1923, as The Meadows Hotel. It still receives favorable reviews.

The renovated Plaza Hotel with restaurant, ballroom, and saloon opened in 1882 as "The Belle of the Southwest." It faces the city's historic Old Town Plaza Park and casts its shadow over the Santa Fe Trail.

These hotels hint at the fascinating ambiance in Las Vegas. A stroll of the streets in any historic district will turn up surprises; a multi-generational family-owned western wear store, a drug store with soda fountain, a small pizzeria in a 140-year-old building

with a two-lane bowling alley, The City of Las Vegas Museum and Rough Rider Memorial, and a delightful little bookstore are but a few examples.

A throwback to the 1950s is the Fort Union Drive In theater. Opened in 1951, it continues to serve the community from April through October.

Dining is as you would expect: unique and diverse. And if you prefer the mundane, the traditional, or just fast food, that, too, is an option.

The best way to discover the array of opportunities in the various historic districts is to get out there and walk around. The Visit Las Vegas website has guides available (www.visitlasvegasnm.com).

The renovated Plaza Hotel with a saloon unchanged from when Doc Holliday bellied up to the bar stands tall on the old Santa Fe Trail.

DISCOVER ALBUQUERQUE

THE EASIEST WAY TO DISCOVER THE best of Albuquerque is to follow the Route 66 corridors. The original alignment of the highway followed 4th Street from north to south. After 1937, it ran east to west along Central Avenue through the historic heart of the city and then up Nine Mile Hill on the climb from the Rio Grande Valley.

The early alignment is amply seasoned with faded relics, quaint neighborhoods of historic homes, and special places. Counted among the latter is the Red Ball Cafe that has been serving the "Wimpy Burger" since 1922.

The Central Avenue corridor on the east and west sides of the historic central business district is a vibrant, swirling blend of modern suburbia made manifest in strip malls, rough old motels with stylish original signage, modern motels, diners and restaurants, old, new, and ethnic, and urban traffic. The central business district is a wealth of old theaters, towering office complexes, decades-old restaurants, and museums.

ABOVE Central Avenue is an exciting blending of modern convenience stores and strip malls, vintage diners and motels, and territorial-era relics.

RIGHT, FROM TOP Built in 1939 by Conrad Hilton the Hotel Andaluz uniquely blends the ambiance of a 1930s luxury hotel with a distinctly Spanish feel.

Many historic motels with original signage remain along the Central Avenue corridor but few have been repurposed or refurbished.

If you do plan on spending a night, a day, or a week in Albuquerque, the Hotel Andaluz located a few blocks off Central Avenue is one recommendation. When it was built in 1939 by Conrad Hilton, it was one of the tallest buildings in the city. During renovation, the unique décor inspired by Spain's Andalusian region was preserved. The rooftop bar and lounge provide breathtaking views of the city and the Rio Grande Valley.

The El Vado Motel, an outstanding example of how an historic building can be repurposed while preserving its originality, is another recommended option. Built in 1937 along Route 66, the *Directory of Motor Courts and Cottages* published by AAA in 1940 notes, "El Vado Courts along the banks of the Rio Grande, five minutes from downtown. Adjoining golf course and bathing beach. 32 units of one to five room apartments. Distinctive Spanish design surrounded by well landscaped grounds. Rates $2.50 to $6 per day."

With the bypass of Route 66 and the building of chain motels, the El Vado began to fade away. Then, it closed and was abandoned.

Recently renovated, including original neon signage, the boutique motel complex offers single rooms or suites. A tap room, swimming pool, and spa are on site. As a bonus, it is less than a fifteen-minute walk from the Albuquerque Biological Park or Historic Old Town with the eighteenth-century San Felipe de Neri Parish and original plaza district.

One attraction in Albuquerque that should not be overlooked is the Sandia Peak Tramway.

The nearly three-mile (4.8 km) tram transports the passenger from the high desert of the Rio Grande Valley to nearly ten thousand feet (3 km) in the Sandia Mountains. The views from the summit or tram are amazing.

The TEN 3 restaurant at the summit offers craft beer, good food, and a truly one-of-a-kind dining experience. Keep in mind that even in the months of summer, it can be a bit chilly on the deck.

Albuquerque is a city rich with museums. Centuries of area history as well as art of the southwest is showcased at the Albuquerque Museum of Art & History in Old Town. Nearby is the New Mexico Museum of Natural History & Science. The city is also home to the National Hispanic Cultural Center, the National Museum of Nuclear Science & History, and the Indian Pueblo Cultural Center.

The Tinkertown Museum is as unique as the city. It is a manifestation of Ross Ward's four-decade passion for wood carving and the collecting of curiosities.

Some walls in the twenty-two-room complex are constructed from tens of thousands of bottles. The outside is a whimsical odyssey through the frontier era in the great American west. A street of false-front buildings is lined with wagon wheels and an astounding array of western memorabilia.

Winding hallways are filled with a staggering array of diverse exhibits: antique tools, coin-operated machines such as Esmeralda the Fortune Teller, a century of "couples" that once adorned wedding cakes, and much, much more. But it is the detailed wood carvings in dioramas, some of which are animated, that are the showstoppers.

A visit to Albuquerque should be savored, not rushed. It is a vibrant, colorful, dynamic cornucopia of blended cultures.

CLOCKWISE FROM TOP LEFT The vibrant historic Old Town District with its galleries, restaurants, and shops on narrow twisting streets is a window into the city's infancy.

Albuquerque promotes its attractions with whimsical signage that blends the city's association with Route 66 and a distinctly New Mexico touch.

The old trading posts at Bernalillo and Dominguez, and ancient pueblos, entranced travelers on the National Old Trails Road and Route 66.

The Route 66 traveler is welcomed to Albuquerque with a colorful arch that hints of the city's rich Native American cultural history.

DRIVE FOUR
TIMELESS WONDERS

THIS LOOP DRIVE IS LESS THAN 175 miles (281.6 km) but even without stops, it would require more than three hours. Highways U.S. 84, State Highways 502 and 4, and U.S. 550 follow the lay of the land through deep canyons, over steep mountains, and along streams and rivers in broad valleys. Only I-25 on the return into Santa Fe runs straight.

This drive back through time is accentuated by stunning landscapes. The first hint that this drive is very special comes just a dozen miles (19.3 km) north of Santa Fe.

The name of the Tesuque Pueblo is a Spanish derivative. The Tewa name is Te Tesugeh Oweengeh, which roughly translates as the "village of the narrow place of the cottonwood trees." The pueblo is world renowned for artisans that create colorful pottery with traditional designs as well as sculpture, clothing, silverwork, and paintings. Listed on the National

ABOVE The Camel Rock formation near the historic Tesuque Pueblo towers above a landscape of rock-strewn hills dotted with cedar and juniper trees.

Register of Historic Places, the pueblo dates to at least 1200 CE.

Nestled along the Rio Grande is the Pueblo de San Ildefonso. It is a relative new-comer as it only dates to about 1300 CE.

In stark contrast to these ancient places is Los Alamos and Los Alamos National Laboratory located a short distance off Highway 4. In the modern era, this was an area of remote ranches in a vast mountain wilderness.

This all changed in 1943. After careful deliberation, the federal government selected the area specifically because of its remoteness to establish a community of scientists to work on the top-secret Manhattan Project, which led to development of the world's first atomic bomb.

The endeavor was so secret that the Los Alamos complex was designated "Site Y."

All residents received their mail through P.O. Box 1663, Santa Fe, New Mexico. After World War II, the laboratory came under the auspices of the Department of Energy and was designated a priority government research facility. It was later named Los Alamos National Laboratory.

Bandelier National Monument is more than 33,000 acres (13354.6 ha) of deeply shadowed canyons, towering mountains that are often capped in snow until late May, and spires of stone weathered into whimsical shapes. Also preserved here are petroglyphs and ancient stone walled villages nestled in deeply shadowed canyons. Some of the archeological sites are estimated to be more than ten thousand years old.

Hiking trails range from wheelchair accessible to strenuous with ladders to access

As storms build over the distant mountains, overlooks such as this one near Los Alamos provide the traveler with panoramic views of a truly awe-inspiring land.

ancient dwellings. Some follow trails worn deep in the stone by the people that once called these canyons home.

Valles Caldera National Preserve in the Jemez Mountains is another find to be uncovered on this drive. Shaded trails lead to streams and small waterfalls, eroded volcanic domes, and hot springs.

Located at the mouth of the breathtaking Canon de Don Diego is the Pueblo of Jemez, one of nineteen pueblos located in New Mexico. This is a vestige of what was once an expansive and highly advanced military state that dates to about 1400 CE. Spanish explorers first contacted the Jemez Nation in 1541. At that time, this was one of largest and most powerful of the Pueblo village networks in the southwest.

Located on high mesa or in deep canyons, fortresses of stone were built, some of which were four stories high with thousands of rooms. The ruins are considered the most expansive interconnected archaeological site in the United States.

Even after crossing the Rio Grande and joining I-25 and sections of Route 66 that were also the ancient El Camino Real, the theme of stunning landscapes, quaint farming villages, ancient pueblos, and imposing archaeological sites continues for the rest of this drive. It encapsulates what makes this "The Land of Enchantment."

I would be remiss if it were not noted that the pueblos and tribes in the southwest are sovereign nations. There are rules of etiquette that with slight variation are universally applicable.

First, stop at the visitor center. They often include a museum or cultural center, and you can inquire about restrictions.

Remember, these villages are not living museums or theme parks. Do not cruise residential districts. As in any community, obey posted traffic, parking, and speed limit signs.

Possession of alcohol, weapons, or drugs is strictly prohibited. Rules may vary but a general rule is that pets are not allowed.

Usually, there are strictly enforced prohibitions on the taking of photographs, visual/audio recording, or sketching, especially during feast days or celebrations. Pueblo Kivas and graveyards are off limits. Traditional Pueblo and tribal dances are religious ceremonies. Observe with quiet reverence and do not applaud.

Do not climb on walls or on other structures. Many are centuries old, and some predate the arrival of Europeans. And never pick up or pocket artifacts.

The Frijoles Canyon trail from Bandelier National Monument to Ponderosa Campground follows a small stream through a canyon with haunting ruins nestled in the walls.

The old trading posts at Bernalillo and Dominguez, and ancient pueblos, entranced travelers on the National Old Trails Road and Route 66.

DRIVE FIVE
FIRE AND ICE

THIS DRIVE FROM GRANTS ALONG
State Highway 53 and U.S. 60 is less than
one hundred miles (190.9 km). It begins
with a pleasant drive along a high desert plain
with colorful mountains looming on the horizon
in all directions. But with abruptness, the plains
give way to a sea of ancient black lava flow
bordered by forested mountains. This is the
El Malpais National Monument.

This is truly an otherworldly place. It seems
to be a blending of forested mountains on earth
and a stark landscape from the moon or Mars.
Sandstone bluffs tower over a frozen sea of con-
torted molten lava. There are stark cinder cones
and lava tubes. Miles of hiking trails traverse the
imposing and harsh landscape providing access to
some of the park's most beautiful places.

Located close by is the privately owned Ice
Cave and Bandera Volcano. Astride the Continental Divide, it is promoted as "The Land of Fire and
Ice." A moderately strenuous trail leads through
a twisted, weathered ancient forest of towering

ABOVE El Malpais National Monument is a study in stark contrasts and a scenic wonderland that often has an otherworldly feel.

ponderosa pines, juniper, and fir trees that have sprouted through the old lava flow. It skirts a dormant volcano and leads to a cave.

Summer or winter, the cave in a lava tube is lined with twisted formations of ice, and in places, layers of ice tinted green by natural artic algae glisten when rays of sunshine reach into the tunnel. It is a study in contrasts.

A hike into and around the Bandera Volcano Crater is unique. There are also breathtaking views of the surrounding mountains and lava flows.

The Ice Caves Trading Post is a throwback to the era of tail fins and "I Like Ike" buttons. Owned by four generations of the Candelaria family, this is a fascinating blending of gift shop with souvenirs and snacks and museum with ancient artifacts and geologic samples.

And a few miles (5 to 6 km) to the west is the towering sandstone bluff that looms over the visitor center at El Morro National Monument. A natural spring at its base has made this an oasis for travelers for centuries. And, it also supported a small village built on the summit around 1275 CE.

Aside from stunning natural beauty, the magic of this national monument centers on this monolith. The two-mile (3.2 km) Headline Trail loop includes the Inscription Trail and then climbs 250 feet (76.2 m) to the summit of the bluff. Sturdy walking shoes and drinking water are a necessity as the trail is steep over uneven sandstone. Aside from the panoramic views of the craters and lava flow of El Malpais and the Zuni Mountains, this trail provides access to El Morro National Monument, the site of Atsinna, an ancient 335-room Puebloan ruin.

The paved half mile (0.8 km) Inscription Trail leads from the visitor center to the springs and pool at the base of the bluff.

Perched high on the summit of the distinctive landmark of El Morro are vestiges of a lost city set against a backdrop of stunning vistas.

This is an amazing outdoor museum filled with centuries of history as well as a natural wonders.

Carved into the soft stone of the grotto at the spring, known as Inscription Rock, are petroglyphs as well as notes and signatures chronicling several hundred years of Spanish and American exploration. Francisco Vasquez de Coronado left a message during his expedition in 1540. There are also notes and names carved to mark the passing expeditions through the rest of the sixteenth century as well as the seventeenth and eighteenth centuries.

The American names carved into the rock read like a who's who of nineteenth-century explorers. The oldest is from artist Richard Kern that is dated September 1849. Pioneers with wagon trains bound for California also left their mark as did Kit Carson and Lt. Edward Fitzgerald Beale who was traveling with his camel corps during the survey expedition for the Beale Wagon Road.

The visitor center built in 1964 should be included as part of a visit to El Morro. On display are exhibits chronicling nearly a thousand years of human history at the site. Here, you will also find information about the trails, camping, and weather conditions.

The drive to Gallup from El Morro is timeless. Little has changed in centuries. Even the sleepy little villages such as Ramah with dusty cafés seem as though they belong to an earlier era.

Please note that some of this drive is through the Ramah Navajo and the Zuni reservations. Each has strictly enforced rules pertaining to photography, and they take speed limits seriously.

Spanning centuries, the inscriptions and petroglyphs carved in the soft stone at El Morro make for a unique glimpse into the past.

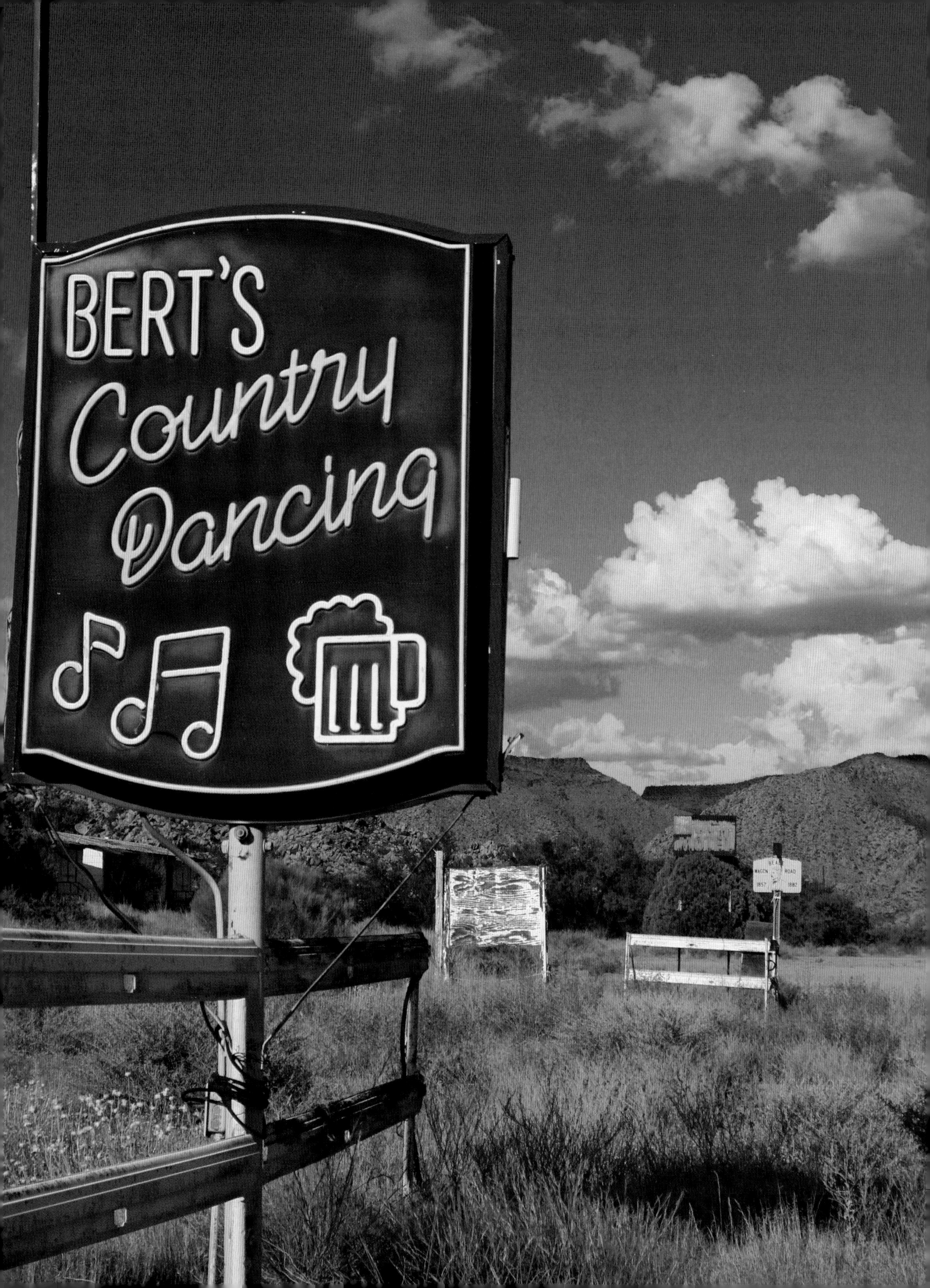
BERT'S
Country
Dancing
WAGON ROAD
1857 1882

Part Seven
ARIZONA

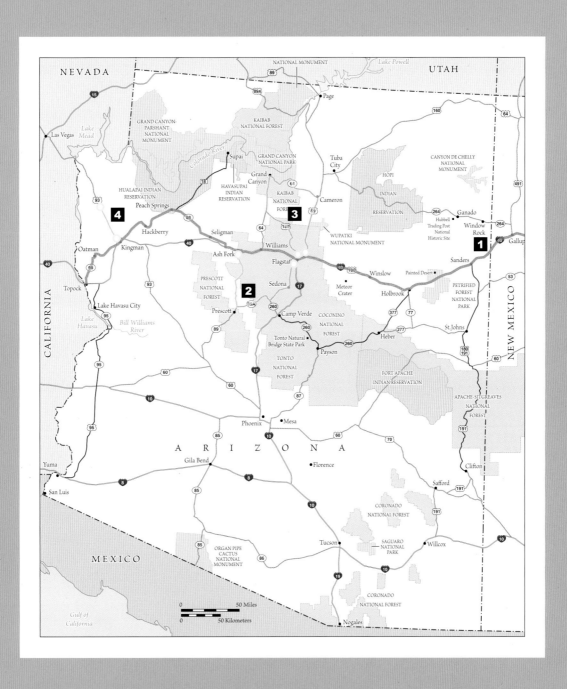

CONSTRUCTION OF I-40 DECIMATED Route 66 in Arizona, except for a very special 160 miles (257.5 km) on the west side of the state. Still, each mile of the storied highway that remains has singular charm. And the drive across the state to the Colorado River on the California state line is also a study in contrast.

On the east is the high desert with juniper- and cedar-studded hills. In the west, the old highway cuts through the Colorado River Valley where the nation's hottest summer temperatures are often recorded. In between is the Painted Desert, the Petrified Forest, and the world's largest ponderosa pine forest in Flagstaff.

The highway crosses into Arizona through a valley bordered by towering stone walls and trading posts, some authentic and some that are classic tourist traps. One on the New Mexico side of the state line was the setting for the 1951 film *Ace in the Hole* starring Kirk Douglas.

ABOVE Route 66 at the Arizona and New Mexico state line is lined with picturesque buttes, colorful walls of stone, and classic tourist traps masquerading as trading posts. **PREVIOUS, LEFT** No one dances at Bert's Country Dancing anymore, but the sign remains as a tangible link to better times.

Route 66 is driven in segments in eastern Arizona, such as from Exit 359 to Exit 354. Each section has its own story to tell.

At Exit 351, just south of the railroad tracks, there is a 1923 bridge that carried Route 66 traffic from 1926 to 1931. At Exit 341, Route 66 is now a graded gravel road that crosses the nearly three hundred-foot (91.4 m)-deep Querino Canyon on a bridge built in 1930.

It isn't drivable today, but Route 66 originally cut across the Petrified Forest National Park. But, you can visit a monument on the old highway during a scenic loop drive through the park. Use Exit 311 and make a stop at the museum and visitor center at the former Painted Desert Inn built in 1924. Continue south through the park to U.S. 180

and then drive to Holbrook where you can again join Route 66.

The devastation wrought by the bypass of Route 66 is evident in Holbrook. But so is the city's vibrant spirit and its colorful frontier heritage.

A few blocks off Route 66, at the intersection of Navajo Boulevard and West Hopi Drive, stands the old stone railroad depot built in 1892. Across the street is the historic Bucket of Blood Saloon and a block of storefronts from the nineteenth century shaded by gnarled old trees.

North of the depot on Joy Nevin Avenue stands the nondescript Blevins House, a private residence, with a street-level historic marker. It was here on September 4, 1887, that Sheriff Commodore Perry Owens

BELOW, CLOCKWISE FROM TOP LEFT On the rim of the canyon spanned by the Querino Canyon Bridge built in 1930 are faint traces of a trading post that was an oasis for Route 66 travelers.

Now a visitor center and museum, the Painted Desert Inn, originally the Stone Tree Inn, was built in 1924 by Herbert Love.

Restored in 2006, the Holbrook railroad depot was built in 1892 to replace a wooden station built by the Atlantic & Pacific Railroad.

The Petrified Forest National Park that includes the stunning beauty of the Painted Desert is the only national park bisected by Route 66.

engaged the Blevins brothers and Andy Cooper in the well-known Owens-Blevins Shootout. It is a surprisingly obscure chapter in western history. But among fans of western history, it, and Owens, are legendary.

On the corner of South Tovar Avenue and West Alvarado Drive is the abandoned Higgins House that in its long history has also been known as the Brunswick Hotel and Arizona Hotel. Built between 1881 and 1883, this is the oldest structure in Holbrook.

The 1898 Navajo County Courthouse, now an intriguing museum, should not be overlooked. The jail in the cellar harkens back to territorial history. Built as a single unit in Missouri and shipped by rail, it was installed during construction.

The courthouse and jail figure prominently in an interesting chapter of Arizona history. George Smiley, an Irish immigrant and railroad worker, was convicted of murder in late 1899. In December, Sheriff Wattron issued an invitation to the hanging that received a presidential reprimand. "You are hereby cordially invited to attend the hanging of one George Smiley, Murderer. His soul will be swung into eternity on Dec. 8, 1899, at 2 o'clock, p.m., sharp. Latest improved methods in the art of scientific strangulation will be employed and everything possible will be done to make the proceedings cheerful and the execution a success."

There are two options for continuing the drive west to Winslow. One is blending Route 66 and I-40 with a drive through Joseph City and a stop at the iconic Jack Rabbit Trading Post that opened in 1949.

Another option is to drive south across the Little Colorado River on U.S. 180, then continue west on Romero Street. Follow the signs to the Holbrook Seventh-day Adventists Indian School. Continue west on McLaws Road and Territorial Road to Highway 99, and then into Winslow.

ABOVE, FROM TOP Now closed, Joe and Aggies Cafe opened at this location on Route 66 in 1965.

Built between 1881 and 1883, the Higgins House that has operated as a hospital, hotel, and dormitory dance hall is purportedly the oldest building in Holbrook.

The old courthouse that serves as a museum houses a diverse array of exhibits including mineral specimens, fossils, petrified wood, and Native America artifacts.

The graded gravel road was the National Old Trails Road and Santa Fe Highway, a predecessor to Route 66. Aside from the stunning desert scenery with whimsical rock formations, the highlight of the drive is the Chevelon Canyon Bridge that spans the chasm of Chevelon Canyon with the beautiful creek far below. Dating late 1912 to early 1913, this was the first highway bridge to be authorized in the state of Arizona.

The bypass of Route 66 decimated the historic business district of Winslow. But as a result of the iconic highway's renewed popularity, it is becoming revitalized as well.

With its mural, statue, and vintage flatbed Ford that illustrates the Eagles first single, "Take It Easy," and oversize Route 66 shield in the intersection, Standin' on the Corner

Park is one of the most photographed locations on Route 66.

The La Posada is the triumph of the city's rebirth. Built in 1929 and added to the National Register of Historic Places in 1992, the restored hotel was once a darling in the Fred Harvey chain.

The fully refurbished Earl's Route 66 Motor Court originally opened in 1953 as the Marble Motel. Another connection to historic Route 66 is the Falcon Restaurant that opened in July 1955.

From Winslow to Winona there is no option but I-40. Route 66 is experienced in the attractions clustered near the exits; the old trading post at Meteor City that is undergoing renovation, the natural wonder that is Meteor Crater, and the haunting ruins of Two Guns framed by the beauty of Canyon Diablo.

Opened in 1913 by the Missouri Valley Bridge & Iron Company, the Chevelon Canyon Bridge was the first to be authorized by the state of Arizona.

The pre-1947 alignment of Route 66 is accessed at Exit 211 at Winona. This scenic highway twists and turns through the ponderosa pine forest, past the old steel-truss Walnut Canyon Bridge, and into Flagstaff.

The later alignment of Route 66 and Highway 622, Walnut Canyon Road, is accessed at Exit 204. Walnut Canyon National Monument is only a few scenic miles (5 to 6 km) south of Route 66. It is an attraction that will enhance a Route 66 odyssey.

Located less than twelve miles (19.3 km) from Flagstaff, Walnut Canyon National Monument is a scenic wonder and an historic site with pre-Columbian history.

Nestled in the walls of Walnut Canyon above Walnut Creek are the ruins of a village that thrived here between 1100 and 1250 CE.

The visitor center with its informative museum on the canyon rim is your portal to this lost world. The one-mile (1.6 km) Island Trail loops through the upper canyon and provides access to some of the pueblo dwellings.

The trail is paved but is not wheelchair accessible. It is considered strenuous because it descends 185 vertical feet (53.4 m) into "the canyon via a series of steep staircases. Even for the physically fit, the hike can be challenging as the trailhead is at seven thousand feet (2.1 km) elevation.

Flagstaff is a dynamic community that is the gateway to the Grand Canyon and Oak Creek Canyon and is the home of Northern Arizona University. And so, the Route 66 corridor is thick with traffic that flows according to the rhythm of a seemingly endless string of traffic lights.

But the crush of traffic is only one throwback to the era when Route 66 was the Main Street of America. Tangible links such as the 1931 Museum Club, a classic roadhouse, the former Du Beau's Motel Inn, opened in 1929, and the 1953 Western Hills Motel abound.

From Flagstaff to Williams, Route 66 is segmented. Some of the old highway is now a graded gravel road. Dusty roadside dinosaurs such as the charming Parks in the Pines general store, circa 1921, fit in perfectly.

Williams has the dubious distinction of being the last Route 66 community to be bypassed by the interstate highway. That was on October 13, 1984.

The historic business district was left empty. That was then. Marketing the city as the gateway to the Grand Canyon and the Route 66 renaissance has transformed the Route 66 corridor into a bustling destination for legions of tourists in every season.

The Grand Canyon Railway that has been operating since 1901 departs from the

Today, Williams, billed as the Gateway to the Grand Canyon, is a vibrant, colorful community that is a destination for travelers in all seasons.

RIGHT, FROM TOP Established in August 1946 by Rodney Graves, Rod's Steak House is one of many historic sites that line the Route 66 corridor in Williams.

No longer operating as a motel, the Copper State Court that was opened by Ezell and Zelma Nelson in 1928 still stands along Route 66 in Ash Fork.

Marooned on a dead-end segment of Route 66 is the charming Partridge Creek Bridge built around 1930.

COPPER STATE COURT, ASH FORK, ARIZONA

Grand Canyon Railway Hotel daily. Noteworthy passengers include presidents Theodore Roosevelt, William Taft, Franklin Delano Roosevelt, and Dwight D. Eisenhower.

Refurbished business along the Route 66 corridor, and some new classics, give the town an infectious vibrancy. The Grand Canyon Hotel that opened in 1891 is one of the oldest continuously operated hotels in the state. The Highlander and Norris Motel both date to 1953. Rod's Steak House opened its doors in 1946. The World Famous Sultana Bar dates to 1912.

I must recommend the Pine Country Restaurant. The food is hearty, delicious, and moderately priced. But for me, the allure begins with a wide variety of tasty, freshly baked pies.

The drive west to Ash Fork with the wonderful Ash Fork Historical Society Museum is on I-40. And after a stop and some exploration, you will again need to take this highway to the Crookton Road exit where you can access nearly 160 uninterrupted miles (257.5 km) of Route 66.

If interested, at Crookton Road, you can cross I-40 and follow a short dead-end segment of Route 66 east for a few miles (5 to 6 km). The highlight of this short drive is the Partridge Creek Bridge built in 1923.

Heading west from the Crookton Road exit, Route 66 crosses a wide plain dotted with cedar and juniper trees. With every mile (1.6 km), it almost seems as though the clock is turning back.

Seligman is credited as the birthplace of the Route 66 renaissance. Decimated by completion of I-40, the Delgadillo family and passionate business owners fought back. The result was designation of Route 66 as a scenic byway and creation of the Historic Route 66 Association of Arizona, the first organization of its kind.

Today, Route 66 enthusiasts consider it a pilgrimage to visit Seligman. A primary focal point is the barbershop of Angel Delgadillo who spearheaded the development of the initiatives that ignited an international fascination with Route 66.

It is easy to walk the town from end to end, and this is the best way to discover its charms such as Historic Seligman Sundries that opened in 1904 or Delgadillo's Snow Cap Drive-In, a whimsical hamburger stand built in 1953.

Refurbished motels such as the 1952 Supai with original neon signage and Deluxe Inn Motel which opened as the Court De Luxe in 1932 are a part of the town's charms.

Seligman at the heart of the Route 66 renaissance is an invigorating blend of whimsy, classic diners, restaurants with an international flair, and a crush of travelers.

Likewise with restaurants such as the Road-kill Cafe and Westside Lilo's.

Westside Lilo's is a family operated business that exemplifies the Route 66 experience in the twenty-first century. The first business in this building was a hobby shop. In the late 1950s, it was remodeled as a restaurant. A few years after completion of I-40 in 1978, business declined precipitously, and the restaurant closed.

Lilo, born in Wiesbaden, Germany, in 1941, married her husband, Patrick Russell, who was stationed at Camp Perry in 1961. In 1996, Lilo and Patrick purchased and remodeled the old restaurant and opened Westside Lilo's. The café is known for hearty American dishes, fresh pastries, and authentic German cuisine.

West of Seligman, Route 66 rolls across the Aubrey Valley where black-footed ferrets and pronghorn antelope still roam free, past a long-closed motel and the ruins of Hyde Park, a complex that once included cabins, a garage and service station, store, and swimming pool. After cresting a cedar-speckled hill, the old highway drops into a small valley bisected by a four-lane segment of Route 66.

When completed at the entrance to Grand Canyon Caverns, this was the only four-lane segment of Route 66 in a rural area between Albuquerque and Los Angeles. At that time, the caverns were the second most visited attraction in the state.

Discovered in 1927, the caverns evolved with Route 66. During the 1950s and 1960s, at the height of popularity, it transformed

BELOW, CLOCKWISE FROM TOP LEFT
Scattered throughout Seligman, away from the theme park atmosphere of the Route 66 corridor, are links to the frontier era such as a bar in a wooden box car.

The Grand Canyon Caverns is a charming blend of classic Route 66 attractions, sculpture, natural wonder, and awe-inspiring landscapes.

The international nature of Route 66 in the 21st century is encapsulated in the welcome, the menu, and the food at Westside Lilo's.

into a resort complex with all the amenities. And after the bypass of Route 66, it also faded, experiencing nearly an 85 percent decline in business. With the highway's rediscovery, it rose from the ashes of neglect like the mythical phoenix.

The motel, pool, café, and gift shop have been refurbished. A restaurant and motel room were added in the cavern itself, and spelunking tours are now available. Paved trails provide access to many attractions in the caverns, and some are wheelchair accessible.

West of the caverns, the highway drops down a steep grade into Peach Springs, headquarters for the Hualapai Reservation. The Hualapai Lodge and Diamond Creek Restaurant represent the modern era. The

shuttered John Osterman Gas Station built in the late 1920s and the Hualapai Forestry offices housed in a trading post built in the early 1920s represent the past.

Diamond Creek Road, an occasionally graded gravel road, provides access to the Colorado River. This is the only vehicular access road that leads to the bottom of the Grand Canyon. Permits are required, and they are available at the lodge. It is recommended that you check on road conditions.

The drive west passes through the mostly abandoned town of Truxton and down Truxton Canyon past the 1880s Crozier Canyon Ranch, a resort complex during the era of National Old Trails Road and the infancy of Route 66. At the bottom of the scenic canyon, before the highway sweeps

The restaurant at Grand Canyon Caverns has been refurbished to its mid-1960s appearance and a café has been added in the caverns.

RIGHT, TOP Truxton is rooted in the past but the faded town dates to 1950, and the founders hope that a proposed dam would spur prosperity.

Keepers of the Wild in a scenic canyon is a recent addition to the roadside that includes ghost towns, historic ranches, and Route 66 relics.

One of the oldest ranches in western Arizona, the Crozier Canyon Ranch was an oasis and resort in the era of the National Old Trails Road and into the 1930s.

A B-17 parked in the shadow of Kingman Army Airfield control tower at an air show seems to be a window into the era of WW II.

7-V Ranch Resort on Highway "66," Arizona
15 miles West of Peach Springs, 38 miles East of Kingman

into the broad Hualapai Valley Mountains, it passes Keepers of the Wild, a wildlife park, the forlorn remnants of the territorial-era Truxton Canyon Indian Agency school complex, the ruins of Valentine, and the iconic Hackberry General Store.

As an historic footnote, the ghost town of Hackberry, located on the south side of the tracks, was a powerhouse in the mid-nineteenth century. At one point, the territorial legislature considered designating it the Mohave County seat.

It is a long straight drive across the valley to Kingman, passing first Stetson Winery and Events Center and then Antares Point Visitor Center and Gift Shop, a former 1964 restaurant that is now dominated by a giant Easter Island–styled head. Most travelers pass the entrance to the Kingman Airport & Industrial Park without a second glance.

In so doing, they are missing something quite special. This airport was established in 1942 as the Kingman Army Airfield. The original air traffic control tower casts its shadow over several monuments commemorating tragedies at the military base and the terminal building that houses The Kingman Airport Café, a wonderful café that serves breakfast and lunch every day.

The airport is also home to Desert Diamond Distillery, manufacturer of award-winning rums and cask-aged whiskeys. A 1918 dining car serves as a restaurant.

Aside from some ancient motels that are now apartments east of Kingman, each mile (1.6 km) driven into town seems to turn back time. Clustered around the interchange with I-40 are modern strip malls, fast food restaurants, motels, and truck stops.

For the first miles west of the interchange, garages, auto dealerships and auto parts stores, and the beautiful Lewis Kingman Park intermingle with motels and restaurants built in the late 1950s and early 1960s. Then, before dropping into the historic heart of the city through the cut in El Trovatore Hill, there are a few motels from the 1929 to 1940 period that today serve as long-term rentals.

Like missing teeth in a beautiful smile, the drive along the Route 66 corridor passes empty lots where motels with brightly shining neon once stood. Those that remain are time capsules. The Ramblin' Rose Motel opened as a Travelodge in 1958, and the iron railings still are adorned with "TL." The Arcadia Lodge, a tarnished gem, dates to 1938. Next door is the circa-1935 White Rock Court, a very rare prewar auto court and the only motel in Kingman listed in the *Negro Motorist Green Book*.

The regeneration in the historic district is most noticeable on Beale Street, one block north of Andy Devine Avenue, Route 66. Bright with glowing neon, a thriving arts district, award-winning microbreweries, wine bars, antique stores, and a diverse array of restaurants with outdoor seating make it well worth a visit.

Chilin' on Beale magnifies that feeling. Held on the third Saturday afternoon of each month, April through October, this fun-filled event is all about vintage cars, hot rods, and music.

The resurgence has not fully reached the Route 66 corridor. The Hotel Beale with a long celebrity association that includes Andy Devine (his father, Thomas, owned the hotel during the early twentieth century), Charles Lindbergh, Buster Keaton, Louis L'Amour, and Amelia Earhart remains closed.

The historic Brunswick Hotel is also empty even though it was recently purchased by a Swiss developer. Sportsman's Club, a territorial-era saloon, Garibaldi's restaurant, and the renovated face of the circa-1915 National Old Trails Garage with a towering 1930 Packard neon sign bode well for the future of the block.

A little further to the west is Dunton Motors established in 1946. This one family–owned business is a museum. And next door is world famous Mr. D'z Route 66 Diner that opened in 1940 as the Kimo Café (KI for Kingman, MO for Mohave County).

The Powerhouse Visitor Center, housed in a powerhouse built in 1907, has two gift shops, the city's tourism office, an exhibit of artwork by Bob Boze Bell, a Route 66 museum, and a fledgling electric vehicle museum. Across the street is Locomotive Park, dominated by a massive 1920s steam-powered Baldwin manufactured locomotive. This has been a rest stop for Route 66 travelers since the 1950s.

On the third Saturday of each month, April through October, Chillin' on Beale, transforms the historic business district into a living time capsule.

A mile (1.6 km) to the north off U.S. 93 is Beale Springs, the basis for Kingman's long transportation history and gateway to the Cerbat Foothills Recreation Area with miles of hiking or mountain biking trails. Camp Beale was established here during the Hualapai Wars in the 1870s. Remnants of a Native American trade route, the territorial-era Mohave Prescott Road, a 1914 highway, and fragments of U.S. 466 are to be found in Coyote Pass.

Route 66 courses west past the Mohave Museum of History & Arts and then through a narrow, scenic canyon into the

An expansive system of trails in the pine-forested Hualapai Mountains and along historic wagon roads in the Cerbat Mountains are among Kingman's treasures.

Sacramento Valley. On the opposite side of the canyon are the pre-1937 alignment of Route 66 and the National Old Trails Road accessed via Fourth Street.

A short distance west of the canyon, Route 66 splits. The post-1952 alignment buried under I-40 heads southwest across the valley past the old Ford proving grounds at Yucca and on to the Colorado River. The earlier alignment that twists and turns through the Black Mountains in Sitgreaves Pass offers miles of scenic wonders and the quasi-ghost town of Oatman where burros have free reign.

Arguably, this is the most scenic section of Route 66. Here, too, are the sharpest curves and steepest grades found anywhere on the highway between Chicago and Santa Monica.

Relics include the rebuilt Cool Springs Station that dates to about 1926, the pastoral ruins of Ed's Camp, the scenic overlook at the site of Snell's Summit Station, Shaeffer's Fishbowl Springs, and the ghost town of Goldroad. Only a few original buildings remain in Oatman, but the town is a booming and fun caricature of a western mining town.

The last miles of Route 66 twist and turn to the Colorado River, past the Havasu National Wildlife Refuge, and the resort at Topock. The graceful arch of the Old Trails Bridge that opened in 1915 still spans the Colorado River. It carried Route 66 traffic from 1926 to 1947, but now carries a natural gas pipeline. It appeared in the 1940 film adaptation of *The Grapes of Wrath* starring Henry Fonda.

Route 66 in Arizona is a technicolor adventure of epic proportions. It is a memory-making odyssey across "The Grand Canyon State."

ABOVE, FROM TOP The pre-1952 alignment of Route 66 through the rugged Black Mountains that cast long shadows across the Colorado River Valley is designated a scenic byway.

Arguably the drive through Sitgreaves Pass is the most dramatically scenic segment of Route 66 between Chicago and Santa Monica.

The Colorado River Valley is a literal desert oasis but in the months of summer temperatures often exceed 120 degrees Fahrenheit (48.9° C), making this the hottest place in the United States.

DRIVE TWO
RED ROCK WONDERLAND

How DO YOU DESCRIBE A DRIVE that includes one of the most picturesque places in America, an opportunity to experience Arizona's back country with a one-of-a-kind train ride, a lively ghost town with million-dollar views, Arizona's territorial capital, and a Route 66 town that is deeply rooted in Arizona territorial history?

This is a drive not to be rushed, even if you could. Google estimates the time for this 145-mile (233.4 km) drive, without stops, to be three hours and thirty minutes.

From downtown Flagstaff, follow South Milton Road to I-17 and Highway 89A. Take the Fort Tuthill County Park exit and continue south on Highway 89A. Be prepared for traffic, a narrow twisting mountain road, and some of the most breathtaking scenery as Rand McNally lists this as one of the top five most scenic drives in the country.

ABOVE A bird's-eye view of Oak Creek Canyon and Slide Rock illustrates why this drive is consistently rated as one of the most beautiful in the United States.

Make use of the many pullouts and picnic areas to savor the stunning views. There are also numerous trailheads as the surrounding hills and canyons are laced with miles of scenic hiking and mountain bike trails.

Nestled in a stunning wonderland of red rock spires is the village of Sedona; this opulent community is a surprisingly inviting blend of opulent Beverly Hills and small-town Arizona. There are resorts, wineries, five-star hotels, steak houses, and galleries, all framed by the breathtaking landscapes.

Tlaquepaque (pronounced T-la-keh-pah-keh), an arts and crafts village on the banks of Oak Creek with quaint cafés, illustrates the unique nature of Sedona. Designed to mimic a traditional Mexican village, towering old sycamore trees shade the twisting cobblestone paths, alleys, and plaza.

Galleries often double as workshops, allowing visitors to watch sculpturers, weavers, glass blowers, painters, or silversmiths create a masterpiece. The artists' village consists of more than fifty shops, galleries, and specialty stores as well as an eclectic array of restaurants or snack bars.

Clarkdale is on old mill town that has been transformed into a destination for visitors as well as people looking for a very special place to call home. Just outside of town is the haunting ruins of Tuzigoot National Monument. Preserved here on a rocky bluff above the vast Verde River Valley are the ruins of what was once a three-story pueblo.

Clarkdale is home to the Verde Canyon Railroad that follows a rail line built in 1912. On this four-hour odyssey, passengers enjoy the beauty of the Verde Canyon from open gondola cars or vintage railcars updated with modern amenities.

Clinging to the steep mountain slopes above the valley along a highway cut into Cleopatra Hill in a series of "Zs" is Jerome, a mining boomtown brought back from the

BELOW The drive from the Ponderosa Pine Forest at Flagstaff, down Oak Creak Canyon and into the red rock wonderland at Sedona is one of the most beautiful drives in America.

BOTTOM Red Rock Crossing on Oak Creek is a quintessential western scene made famous in countless cinematic epics.

abyss of abandonment by visionaries and ambitious entrepreneurs. Established in 1876, Jerome once claimed a population of more than fifteen thousand people when mine production peaked at three million pounds (1,360,777 kg) of copper each month.

With closure of the Phelps Dodge Mine in 1953, the town entered a period of precipitous decline. Before the revitalization in the 1980s, the population had plummeted to fewer than one hundred people.

Today, with a population of almost five hundred people, the old town is promoted as Arizona's liveliest ghost town. Galleries,

restaurants, and quirky hotels such as the Jerome Grand Hotel housed in the expansive former mining company hospital ensure a memorable and fun visit with million-dollar views of the Verde Valley.

Explosive growth in recent years has transformed Prescott into a modern mini metropolis. But its spirit hearkens to the territorial era when this was the Arizona capital and the early years of statehood.

The Yavapai County Courthouse, built in 1916, is set at the center of lush Courthouse Square, often used for art or musical festivals. It is at the nucleus of a vibrant historic district, including Whiskey Row, named after the many old west saloons that are found along this downtown block.

The crème de la crème of historic watering holes is The Palace Saloon. Established in 1877, this ornate delight is the oldest continuously operated saloon in Arizona. Before their illustrious exploits in Tombstone, Wyatt Earp, Virgil Earp, and Doc Holliday were frequent patrons of the saloon as Virgil owned a sawmill at Thumb Butte and served as the Prescott constable.

A few blocks away is the Sharlot Hall Museum complex. Counted among the many historic buildings on the site is the territorial governor's mansion, a two-story log cabin built in 1864.

The historic district is best explored on foot as traffic congestion and parking can present a challenge. This is made easier as the historic district has four renovated historic hotels, each a showpiece; the Hassayampa Inn built in 1927, the Grand Highland Hotel, a newly reconstructed circa-1903 hotel, Hotel Vendome built in 1917, and the Hotel St. Michael that opened in 1891.

Some of the charm has gone out of the drive to Ash Fork on Highway 89 through Chino Valley and Paulden as urban sprawl and traffic congestion on the narrow old highway makes it difficult to relax and enjoy the sites. Still, there are ample pullouts and opportunity to experience quaint old diners, scenic views, and vestiges from early times such as a beautiful old bridge spanning Hells Canyon.

Ash Fork has seen better days. That is obvious from the nearly empty streets, closed-up buildings, and weathered storefronts. But this town is not dead. In fact, it is chock-full of surprises such as LuLu Belle's BBQ, a delightful restaurant.

The sense of history is palpable, and for good reason. The confluence of the three tributaries of Ash Creek was a favored resting

BELOW Watson Lake in the beautiful Granite Dells north of Prescott is a highlight of the drive to Ash Fork, and in summer is a wonderful place for a picnic.

BOTTOM With several renovated and well-preserved historic hotels, it is easy to enjoy the vibrant nightlife of Prescott's world-famous Whiskey Row.

place for travelers on a pre-Columbian trade route as well as for Spanish and American explorers. It was this dependable source of water that led the Atlantic & Pacific Railroad to establish a camp at this site in 1882.

Historians generally consider completion of a rail line from Phoenix to the junction at Ash Fork in 1895 as the end of the frontier era in Arizona. Aside from the railroad, the National Old Trails Road and Route 66 also contributed to the town's prosperity. Indications of this lengthy history are scattered throughout the sleepy town.

Exploration of Ash Fork begins with a visit to the Ash Fork Route 66 Museum. It is housed in a building built in the 1920s by the railroad as a repair and maintenance facility.

This loop drive seems to have it all. Scenic wonders, history, fine dining, Route 66, ghost towns, historic saloons, and an opportunity for mile after mile of smile-inducing adventures.

DRIVE THREE
THE GRAND LOOP

THIS IS A DRIVE THAT EXEMPLIFIES the diversity of Arizona. On the drive north along U.S. 89, the often-snow-capped San Francisco Peaks serve as a backdrop to a plain that sweeps into the Painted Desert. East and south along State Highway 64 is through a high desert plain that gives way to forest and deep canyons, including the grandest canyon of all, the Grand Canyon. And then, on U.S. 180 back into Flagstaff, the drive is through high country where the mountains are framed by white aspen.

The first stop on this odyssey is at Sunset Crater Volcano National Monument. Created about nine hundred years ago, the one thousand-foot (308.4 m)-high Sunset Crater cinder cone towers over a landscape of old lava flows and cinder fields shaded by towering ponderosa pines.

Begin with the informative and fascinating visitor center. Here, you will find information

ABOVE Timelessness is the theme of this drive; centuries-old ruins framed by stark desert plains, trading posts from the western frontier, and canyons created by thousands of years of erosion.

about the various hiking trails that provide access to the park's secrets and its most scenic locations.

If time is limited, I suggest the relatively easy one-mile (1.6 km) Lava Flow Trail. This walk along the base of Sunset Crater Volcano provides expansive views of the old lava flow and the forest that has sprouted from the moon-like landscape.

The next stop is Wupatki National Monument. Towering and expansive pueblos built of red stone sprawling on hills between the ponderosa-covered slopes of the San Francisco Peaks and the Painted Desert are at the center of this park.

Hikes range from relatively easy on paved trails to wilderness adventures such as the Crack in Rock hike. This is a twenty-mile (32.2 km), two-day guided backpacking trip to the hauntingly beautiful ruins of a circa-

twelfth-century pueblo sitting high on a mesa. The hike is through a harsh landscape of broken and weathered stone, cinder fields, and sandy plains.

A highlight of a visit to Cameron is the Cameron Trading Post that opened in 1916, five years after the suspension bridge was erected over the Little Colorado River Gorge. It was established by two brothers, Hubert and C.D. Richardson, that bartered Hopi and Navajo livestock, handicrafts, wool, and woven blankets for dry goods.

Built of hand-cut red sandstone, the trading post seems as timeless as the landscape. Housed in the old trading post with its large stone fireplace and vintage pressed tin ceiling is the Grand Canyon Restaurant, an excellent place to savor a meal while enjoying views of the Little Colorado River Gorge.

The first opportunity to view the majestic wonder of the Grand Canyon is at Desert View Watchtower in Desert View within Grand Canyon National Park. From there to Grand Canyon Village is a twenty-five-mile (40.2 km) scenic drive along a section of Highway 64 known as Desert View Drive. Highlights include six developed canyon viewpoints that offer different perspectives of the canyon, four picnic areas, several pull-outs along the canyon rim, and the Tusayan Museum and Ruin that includes the remains of an ancient pueblo.

Grand Canyon Village with a population of just over two thousand people is the heart of the park's service industry. It dates to 1901 when the first train from Williams, Arizona, arrived on the recently completed spur line. Within ten years, the village had grown from a few cabins and a company that offered mule rides to the bottom of the canyon to a mul-tifaceted complex that included a rustic log train depot and the majestic El Tovar Hotel, gift shops, and galleries on the canyon rim.

As a point of interest, this is one of the oldest wooden train depots in the United States that is still in use. And the Grand Canyon Railway still offers daily service from Williams.

On the drive south, a few miles (5 to 6 km) from Tusayan, the landscape changes dramatically from thick ponderosa pine forests to the Coconino Plateau, a rolling open plain peppered with cedar and juniper. Valle, also known as Grand Canyon Junction, at the junction of Highway 64 and U.S. 180, is home to Planes of Fame Air Museum, an attraction well worth a visit.

On the drive into Flagstaff, the prairies quickly give way to pine forest, and as you climb in elevation, to white aspen. You will also pass the entrance to Arizona Snowbowl, a premier ski resort that also offers an array of summer activities including gondola rides. Be sure to make a stop at the Humphrey Peak Lookout; the views are stunning and not at all what most people expect to see in Arizona.

Located a few miles (5 to 6 km) from Flagstaff is the historic Lowell Observatory. The foundation of this historic observatory was laid in 1896 when astronomer Percival Lowell contracted internationally acclaimed telescope makers Alvan Clark & Sons to build a 24-inch (61 cm) refractor telescope.

This loop drive is a bit long, nearly 250 miles (402.3 km). But rest assured, the rewards are colorful and unforgettable memories are made with each mile (1.6 km).

BELOW Opened in 1905, the El Tovar Hotel on the rim of the Grand Canyon with gift shop, dining room, and lounge has hosted celebrities and presidents.

BOTTOM For the traveler not familiar with Arizona's diverse landscapes, Lockett Meadow, and the mountains that serve the Arizona Snowbowl, are a forested surprise.

DRIVE FOUR
THE WESTERN FRONTIER

THIS IS ANOTHER SHORT DETOUR, JUST twenty-five miles (40.2 km) each way. Simply head north on U.S. 93, then hang a right on County Highway 125 and follow the signs to Chloride. But to get the most from this adventure, I suggest you bring along a pair of hiking boots.

To set the mood, just as you pass a string of truck stops and generic fast food restaurants, look for Fort Beale Drive on the right side of the highway. Follow this for about a mile (1.6 km) to the parking lot and monuments at Beale Springs. The one hundred-yard (91.4 m) trail is an easy hike.

Surrounded by towering buttes, this desert oasis with its ruins and gnarled mesquite trees is a delightful place for a picnic. A short loop trail takes you past several kiosks that note the site of historic structures including a ranch house built in the 1890s and the buildings that constituted the military outpost of Camp Beale Springs.

ABOVE The trails in the Cerbat Foothills Recreation area lead to scenic overlooks, a hidden desert oasis, colorful canyons, gardens of stone, and historic sites.

During the Hualapai Wars of the 1870s, this camp was built to safeguard a key transportation corridor in northwestern Arizona. This was also the site of the first reservation for the Hualapai people before they were force-marched to the Colorado River.

A trailhead accessed via Fort Beale Drive, about a mile (1.6 km) from Beale Springs, is your gateway to the miles of scenic trails in the Cerbat Foothills Recreation Area. Some of these trails parallel U.S. 93 in Coyote Pass as they follow historic roads: the mid-nineteenth-century Mohave Prescott Toll Road, a highway built in 1914, and U.S. 466.

One of the trails crosses under U.S. 93 and leads into a valley of weathered and twisted rock formations known as Monolith Gardens. It has been described as a miniature Monument Valley.

The trails range from moderate to strenuous. Aside from hiking, they are ideal for mountain biking. There are springs and awe-inspiring views of the Hualapai Mountains, Kingman, and the Sacramento Valley.

The drive to Chloride is relatively mundane as it is a four-lane highway that is often clogged with traffic en route to Las Vegas. Only the majestic Cerbat Mountains infuse the drive with a sense of excitement and wonder.

The Cerbat Foothills Recreation Area with easily accessed trailheads offers miles of scenic trails through stunning landscapes in the Cerbat Mountains.

Chloride still has a pulse, barely. On the main streets there is a delightful café, Yesterday's Restaurant and Shep's Miners Inn, and a bar as well as some charming old storefronts. The few hundred residents live in trailers and miners' cabins, leftovers from the town's peak years. Discovering tarnished gems such as the old Arizona & Utah Railroad depot is the reward for slowly driving the side streets.

Dating to the 1860s, Chloride is one of the oldest continuously inhabited mining towns in the state of Arizona. The town, nestled in the foothills of the towering Cerbat Mountains, boomed in the years bracketing 1900.

The Arizona & Utah Railroad provided daily service to the junction with the main line of the Santa Fe Railroad at McConnico. There were hotels, saloons, general stores, restaurants, a stock exchange, and mining companies

Today, it is a sleepy village of retirees that savor the solitude and privacy. And, it is a tangible link to Arizona territorial history as well as a place to enjoy great pie and coffee.

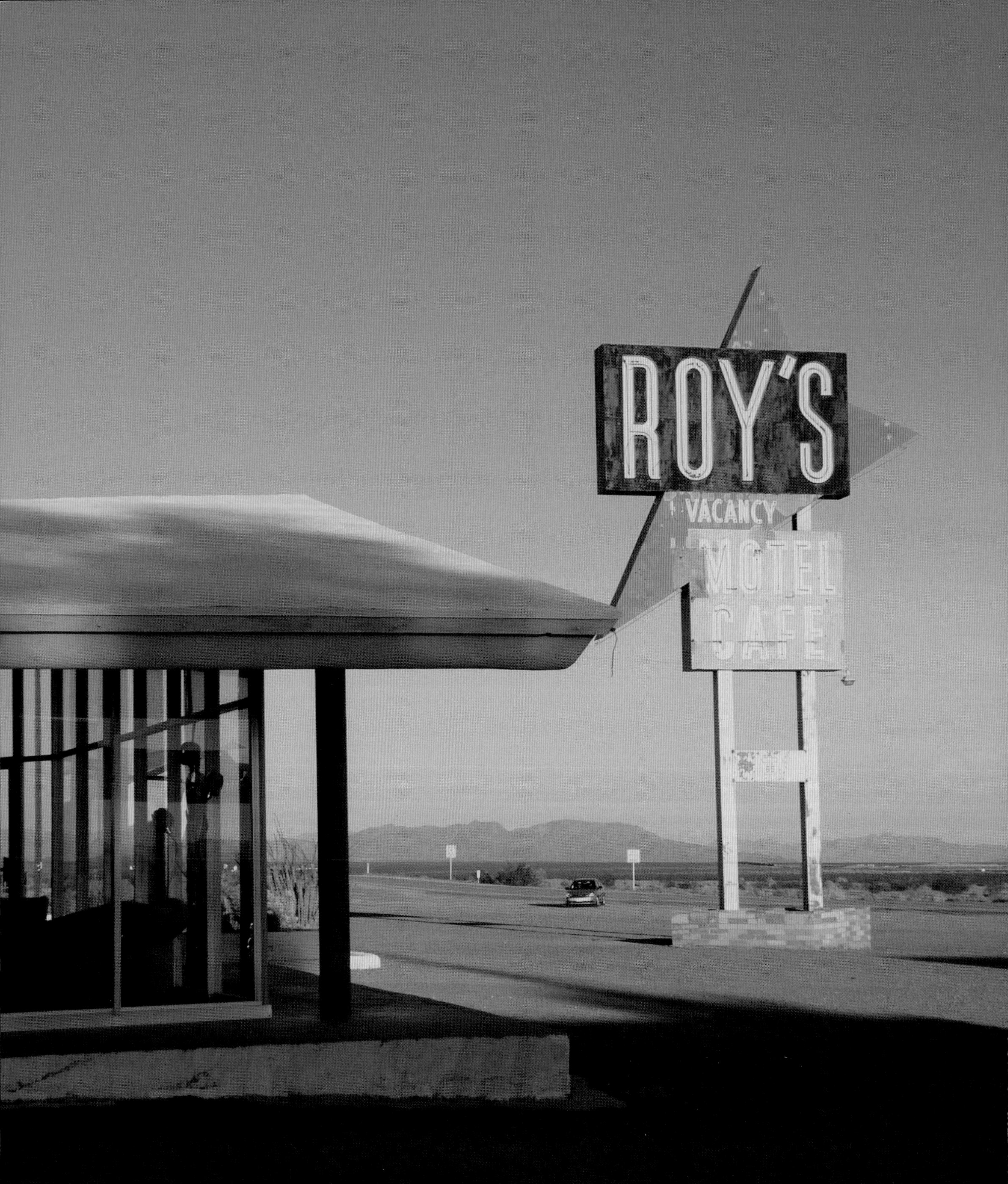
ROY'S
VACANCY
MOTEL
CAFE

Part Eight
CALIFORNIA

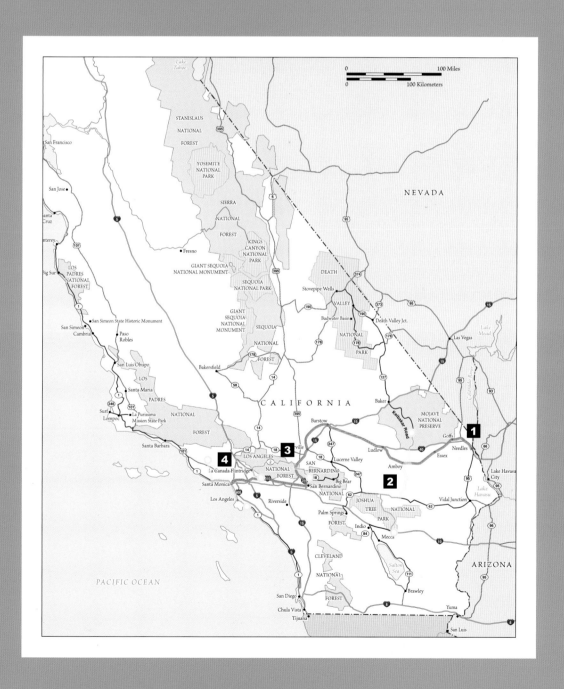

R OUTE 66 IN CALIFORNIA IS A STUDY in diversity. It crosses the vast wilderness of the Mojave Desert. And, it traverses one of the largest metropolises in the United States. It cuts through ghost towns and the core of the historic Los Angeles Theatre District. It links the desert oasis of the Colorado River Valley and the Pacific Ocean.

Between the Colorado River and Needles, there are portions of the old highway that can be accessed from the Park Moabi exit. They are now dead-end roads, but each section has interesting mementos from the highway's halcyon days.

Needles has been decimated, first by relocation of Santa Fe Railroad operations and then with the bypass of Route 66. But the old town is resilient.

Fender's River Road Resort is another throwback. Dating to about 1960, it is the only motel and RV park located on the Colorado River, National Old Trails Road, and Route 66.

Dominating the square is the old El Garces railroad hotel. Built in 1908, it is being

ABOVE Replaced by construction of I-40 this former railroad bridge dated to the late 19th century and carried Route 66 traffic after 1947.
PREVIOUS, LEFT By the 1950s the never-ending flow of traffic on Route 66 kept a string of cafés, garages, and diners open twenty-four hours a day in Amboy.

refurbished and currently operates as a local event and community center.

West of Needles to the junction of Highway 95, Route 66 has been buried under I-40. But if you follow Highway 95 north to State Highway 66, you can access the earliest alignment of the iconic old highway and follow it through Goffs to Fenner. This is the course of the National Old Trails Road and the Arrowhead Highway that connected Los Angeles to Salt Lake City before creation of the U.S. Highway System.

Fenner, never more than a wide spot in the road, is just a truck stop in the desert. Goffs is largely a vacant ghost town except for the old schoolhouse that is now the Mojave Desert Heritage and Cultural Association.

The quality of this museum in the middle of nowhere is the first surprise. The second is the diversity of exhibits inside as well as on the expansive grounds and the passion of the volunteers that keep it in repair and open.

Route 66 crosses I-40 at Fenner. But resultant of a washed-out bridge, it dead ends a few miles (5 to 6 km) from the desert-bleached town of Essex.

At Exit 78, Kelbaker Road, you can again access Route 66 with a twelve-mile (19.3 km) drive. A left turn allows you to follow the old highway east to the ruins at Chambless and

CLOCKWISE FROM LEFT At the Highway 95 crossing of the Colorado River stands a monument commemorating where the National Old Trails Road entered California.

This is the literal crossroads of history in Needles, where the National Old Trails Road and Route 66 entered Needles from the east.

The original alignment of Route 66 followed the course of the National Old Trails Road along the railroad tracks and around the plaza at the El Garces.

It is surprising to find a museum such as the Mojave Desert Heritage and Cultural Association with detailed and expansive exhibits in a ghost town.

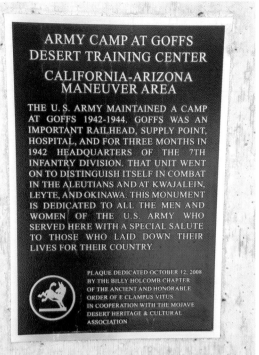

ARMY CAMP AT GOFFS
DESERT TRAINING CENTER

CALIFORNIA-ARIZONA
MANEUVER AREA

THE U.S. ARMY MAINTAINED A CAMP
AT GOFFS 1942-1944. GOFFS WAS AN
IMPORTANT RAILHEAD, SUPPLY POINT,
HOSPITAL, AND FOR THREE MONTHS IN
1942 HEADQUARTERS OF THE 7TH
INFANTRY DIVISION. THAT UNIT WENT
ON TO DISTINGUISH ITSELF IN COMBAT
IN THE ALEUTIANS AND AT KWAJALEIN,
LEYTE, AND OKINAWA. THIS MONUMENT
IS DEDICATED TO ALL THE MEN AND
WOMEN OF THE U.S. ARMY WHO
SERVED HERE WITH A SPECIAL SALUTE
TO THOSE WHO LAID DOWN THEIR
LIVES FOR THEIR COUNTRY.

PLAQUE DEDICATED OCTOBER 12, 2008
BY THE BILLY HOLCOMB CHAPTER
OF THE ANCIENT AND HONORABLE
ORDER OF E CLAMPUS VITUS
IN COOPERATION WITH THE MOJAVE
DESERT HERITAGE & CULTURAL
ASSOCIATION

CLOCKWISE FROM TOP LEFT Little remains in Amboy aside from a long-shuttered motel and school, a forlorn church, a service station, and a post office.

The establishment of a vast military training center in the Mojave Desert gave Goffs a brief respite in its fade to ghost town.

Only a clearing in the desert, some debris, and a surprisingly well-maintained cemetery mark the site of the desert oasis that was Bagdad.

Cadiz Summit before reaching the washout. Turn west and you can follow the double six through Amboy, past the site of Bagdad, and into Ludlow.

This is the middle of the Mojave Desert. The long-vanished oasis of Bagdad holds a dubious record. According to railroad records, between October 3, 1912, and November 8, 1914, not one drop of rain fell. This is an unofficial record for lack of precipitation.

There are no traces of Amboy's early years before the American Civil War when there were salt harvesting operations in the area. In fact, aside from the gas station, a long-closed school, motel with its towering Roy's sign, and the post office, almost nothing remains of a booming town where garages, gas stations, and restaurants never closed.

From the roadside rest area to Amboy Crater is a short loop hike of three miles (4.8 km) through a harsh landscape of sand, an old lava flow, and cinders and into the crater through a breech. Another trail leads to the summit where you can hike the rim.

It should be noted that is a desert wilderness where summer temperatures often exceed 120 degrees Fahrenheit (48.9°C). Even in the months of winter, temperatures can reach into the 90s (over 32°C). Always carry water, and always let someone know when you plan to return. In the past few years, several tourists have died along this trail.

Ludlow is another faded town. There are a couple of gas station mini marts, the Ludlow Cafe, and the Ludlow Motel. And the motel is an oddity as you check in at the Chevron gas station across the street.

But just two blocks behind the café, along the railroad tracks, is ample evidence that this was a thriving community. Sidewalks, stairs that go nowhere, and tumble-down buildings are all that remain of a town that was once an important railroad junction, suppling the needs of travelers on the Arrowhead Highway, National Old Trails Road, and Route 66, and a supply center for area mines.

Aside from the old Bagdad Cafe, Newberry Springs is another sun-bleached desert town whose best years are now a distant memory. But because of the springs that make this a desert oasis, there is a history here that spans centuries.

There is archeological evidence that it was used by travelers on a Native American trade route for a thousand years. European association with the spring dates to the expeditions of Father Francisco Garces in 1776.

FROM TOP The trail from the picnic area and parking lot at Amboy Crater National Natural Landmark provides unique access to a volcanic crater and panoramic views from the rim.

Located on the National Old Trails Road and the Arrowhead Highway, and at an important railroad junction, Ludlow boomed in the years bracketing WW I.

Even relics such as this long shuttered garage are becoming a rarity in Ludlow as they succumb to the harsh elements and vandalism.

Daggett is another weathered holdover from the frontier era. The long-closed Stone Hotel dates to the late 1870s. It has a direct connection to naturalist John Muir and the infamous "Death Valley Scotty." And, there is persistent legend that it may also be linked to Wyatt Earp.

But not everything in Daggett is closed, abandoned, or just pictorial ruins. The Desert Market has been in continuous operation since opening as Ryerson's General Store in 1908.

Just as in the era of Route 66, the flow of traffic on two major Highways, I-40 and I-15, ensures Barstow doesn't follow the course of other desert communities along the old highway. Added economic support comes from the Marine Corps Logistics

FAR LEFT, TOP Dating to the 1920s, little remains of the Cliff House complex that included a gas station, café, cabins, store, post office, and terminal for Greyhound and Continental Trailways bus companies.

FAR LEFT, BOTTOM

LEFT, TOP Built in 1947 from discarded railroad ties and other salvaged materials, the El Rancho faces an uncertain future as evidence mounts that it is not being maintained.

LEFT, BOTTOM The nondescript, derelict remains of the Stone Hotel and a weathered storefronts are tangible links to more than 140 years of history in Daggett.

Base established during World War II.

Along the Route 66 corridor are numerous reminders of the highway's glory days. Just one example is the El Rancho Motel built by Cliff Chase in 1947 who used discarded ties from the defunct Tidewater & Tonopah Railroad in its construction.

A highlight of a Barstow visit is the Casa del Desierto, a Harvey House hotel complex built between 1909 and 1910. Today, two museums are housed in this historic building: the Western America Railroad Museum and the Route 66 "Mother Road" Museum.

To drive Route 66 between Barstow and Victorville is to experience the highway as it was in the 1950s, apart from a crush of traffic and the businesses that are closed and weathered. One of the most interesting sights on this desert drive is the bridge spanning the Mojave River.

This is the only steel-truss bridge of this type on Route 66 in California. Built in 1932, it retains its original ornate iron work guardrail on the approaches.

Victorville was also established as a railroad town. But the history predates the town by decades as the Spanish Trail passed through this valley along the Mojave River.

Route 66 landmarks and attractions as well as a site associated with Hollywood history make Victorville unique among Route 66 communities. On a westbound trip, the first of these encountered is Emma Jean's Holland Burger Cafe, opened in 1947, and was featured in several television shows and movies.

The California Route 66 Museum is in Victorville, as is the forlorn old Green Spot Motel that was once part of a resort complex. Popular with Hollywood elite as well as for actors filming movies in the area, the motel has a direct connection

ABOVE FROM TOP
The railroad, the National Old Trails Road, and then Route 66 ensured that downtown Barstow was vibrant, busy, and prosperous.

Listed on the National Register of Historic Places, the repurposed Casa del Desierto is an architectural gem that is a tangible link to the city's railroad history.

GREEN SPOT MOTEL Victorville, Calif. 44108 Housh-Corona

to what many think is one of the greatest movies ever made. In 1940, Herman Mankiewicz and John Houseman stayed at the Green Spot while writing the first drafts for the movie *Citizen Kane.*

Decades of highway construction have decimated large swaths of Route 66 and businesses along that highway in the Cajon Pass. But the sections that remain are delightful drives. It should be noted that for centuries, this pass has funneled traffic from the coastal plains into the high desert.

I will delve more into the attractions in the Los Angeles metropolitan area and share side trips for enjoying Route 66 in drive four. Concerns about traffic and crime, real and perceived, prevent many from following the old highway from San Bernardino to Santa Monica. As a result, this is one of the most overlooked segments of Route 66 and one of the most fascinating.

DRIVE TWO
THE CALDRON

CAJON PASS 4010

THIS IS TWO DRIVES WITH AMBOY AS the center point. One drive is north forty miles (64.4 km) to the old town of Kelso in the Mojave National Preserve. The other is fifty miles (80.5 km) south to Twentynine Palms, gateway to the Joshua Tree National Park. Every mile (1.6 km) is through foreboding, empty, vast, and scenic desert landscapes that are best enjoyed in late fall or early spring.

The sprawling 1.6-million-acre (647,497 ha) Mohave National Preserve is a wonderland of towering sand dunes that sound as though they are singing when the wind blows, otherworldly Joshua tree forests, volcanic cinder cones, and limitless horizons.

For the truly adventuresome, the historic Mojave Road traverses the preserve as it connects the Colorado River Valley to a point near Wilmington, California at I-15. Most of this nearly 150-mile (241.4 km) road is not maintained and, as some sections are rocky or sandy, a four-wheel drive vehicle is a must. The road was first developed as a trade route trail connecting tribes in present-day Arizona and New Mexico with the

ABOVE The Mohave National Preserve is a wonderland of sand dunes, ghost towns, scenic wonders, and a 19th-century road that is a destination for legions of off-road enthusiasts.

Chumash and other coastal tribes. As it connected springs and dependable sources of water in the desert, it was also followed by Spanish and American explorers.

In the mid-nineteenth century, it was developed as a government road and remained a primary desert crossing until completion of the railroad in the 1880s. Military outposts were established at regular intervals to protect vital sources of water and to provide valuable services for travelers. It was largely an historic footnote until the 1980s when Dennis Casebier published *The Mojave Road Guide*.

The visitor center for the Mohave National Preserve that also includes an informative museum is housed in the 1924 Spanish Mission–styled railroad depot, Kelso Depot. Renovated in 2005, it is one of the few remaining traces of the railroad town of Kelso.

The drive south from Amboy on the Amboy Road is past desolate salt harvesting operations and the Cleghorn Lake Wilderness Area and over the barren Sheep Hole Mountain. The expansive views are awesome.

Twentynine Palms is a small but modern community that thrives as the gateway to Joshua Tree National Park. It is also home to the Marine Corps Air Ground Combat Center established in early 1942 as the Twentynine Palms Air Academy, a glider training airfield used by the Army Air Corps.

Attractions in Twentynine Palms are diverse. Pioneertown is a preserved movie set built by Roy Rogers for use in the filming of western films during the 1940s. According to the Morongo Basin Historical Society, Pioneertown's six-lane Pioneer Bowl bowling alley, used by the film crews and actors, is the oldest one in the Morongo Basin.

The General Patton Memorial Museum is located at the site of former Camp Young near the southern entrance to Joshua Tree National Park. This was a base for the sprawling desert warfare training center established by General Patton in 1942 as he prepared troops for the invasion of North Africa. Aside from displays about the desert training center, there are exhibits that chronicle Patton's military career and an array of tanks that

BELOW, CLOCKWISE FROM TOP LEFT The mid-19th-century Mojave Road and other old trails across the forbidding but picturesque Mojave Desert are popular with off-road enthusiasts.

When it opened in 1924 the Los Angeles & Salt Lake Railroad depot at Kelso included a telegraph office, dormitory rooms for staff, a billiard room, and lunch counter.

Pioneertown was established in 1946 by Dale Evans, Roy Rogers, and other investors as a movie set and attraction that mimicked an 1880s western frontier town.

General Patton, credited with establishment of the Desert Training Center in preparation for the invasion of North Africa, is honored at General Patton Memorial Museum located in the Mojave Desert.

OPPOSITE Establishment of Joshua Tree National Monument in 1936, an 825,000-acre desert wonderland, is credited to Minerva Hoyt's work to thwart cacti poachers.

chronicle their evolution from World War II through the Vietnam War.

Preserved at Joshua Tree National Park is the junction of two distinct desert ecosystems: the Mojave and the Colorado. If your schedule is limited, or you prefer to experience some of the park's wonders without hiking, horseback riding, or a backroad 4 × 4 adventure, consider the eighteen-mile (29 km) motor tour on the Geology Tour Road. This will provide access to some of the park's most iconic locations.

A simple hike that I recommend is the one-mile (1.6 km) loop trail along an old road to the crumbling adobe ruins of Ryan Ranch. It was built in the closing years of the nineteenth century by J. D. Ryan, owner of the Lost Horse Mine. Originally,

it consisted of a main house with a veranda, a bunkhouse, barn, and various outbuildings. Maps to this and other sites are available at the visitor center.

This is a trip best made in early spring or late fall. Summer temperatures often exceed 110 degrees Fahrenheit (43.3°C). And it may surprise first-time desert visitors to learn that during the winter, temperatures can plummet to freezing or lower.

Regardless of season, make sure to carry water. If you don't need it, you might find someone who does, and there is little to no cell service in much of this area. And remember, take nothing but photographs and leave nothing but footprints.

DRIVE THREE
THE HIGH ROAD

THIS DRIVE FROM CAJON JUNCTION IN the Cajon Pass to the Saga Motor Hotel built in 1957 along Route 66 in Pasadena is short, a mere eighty-five miles (136.8 km). But the Angeles Crest Scenic Byway, consistently recognized as one of the most beautiful drives in California, will require at least two hours, if you can resist the urge to stop at pullouts and enjoy the stunning scenery. And as the crest at Dawson Saddle is nearly eight thousand feet (2,438.4 m), this is also one of the highest highways in the state of California.

It begins with State Highway 138 north through Cajon Pass. Keep your eyes open for the visible fault lines as some of this drive is over the San Andreas Fault.

At Mountain Top Junction, turn west onto State Highway 2, the Angeles Crest Scenic Byway. From the junction, it is sixty-six miles (106.2 km) to La Cañada Flintridge. In between is just one community, Wrightwood.

A group of Los Angeles–area businessmen and community leaders began soliciting support for construction of "the most scenic and picturesque

ABOVE One of the most beautiful drives in California, Angeles Crest Highway is an engineering marvel that with each mile provides the driver stunning views.

mountain road in the state" along the highest and most scenic ridges of the San Gabriel Mountain range in 1912. The organization they formed, in partnership with the state of California, received an allocation of funds to begin construction in 1919.

Actual work on the scenic highway didn't commence until 1929. Except for the World War II years, work was continuous and yet it wasn't completed until 1956. Check on road conditions in the forested village of Wrightwood as the highway has occasionally closed resultant of landslides and fire restrictions.

Wrightwood at an elevation of 5,935 feet (1809 m) is quite an oasis after crossing the desert. And as it is a ski town, it is a popular destination for residents throughout southern California in any season. There is an array of wonderful restaurants and lodging options.

The road was considered an engineering feat. Record deep cuts, one is 240 feet (73.2 m), in granite were required. To keep the highway above deep canyons and chasms, tunnels were also needed.

Aside from scenic pullouts, rest areas, and picnic sites, this highway and Highway 39 also provide access to miles of wilderness trails. One of the more intriguing hikes in the San Gabriel Mountains is the trail to the Bridge to Nowhere, about ten miles (16.1 km) in length, accessed from Highway 39 just south of its junction with the Angeles Crest Highway.

The arch bridge that towers over the East Fork of the San Gabriel River was built in 1936 as part of a highway construction project to link Azusa with Wrightwood. Extensive flooding in 1938 destroyed most of the highway that had been built but

the bridge survived, and the project was abandoned.

With startling abruptness, the highway landscape changes from mountain wilderness to urban sprawl at La Cañada Flintridge. In the span of five minutes, you pass from beautiful views of Los Angeles to stoplights and a crush of traffic.

The destination for this drive is the Saga Motor Hotel, a classic mid-1950s motel that is so well preserved it is often used as a set for movie and television production companies. Surrounding the swimming pool are towering palm trees, and the courtyard preserves a stereotypical view of mid-1950s California.

As a bonus, there is an array of fascinating restaurants within walking distance along Colorado Boulevard. Exemplifying the diversity would be Heidar Baba and Lucky Baldwins Trappiste Pub.

Heider Baba is an authentic Persian café. The menu is rich with fascinating taste treats such as mast-o khiar, yogurt with cucumber as an appetizer, and koobideh, skewers of seasoned ground lamb and grated onion that are cooked over an open fire and served with delicious basmati rice and grilled tomato and chili.

Lucky Baldwins Trappiste Pub is a British pub–style restaurant. Aside from more than sixty beers on tap, the menu offerings are authentic British pub offerings such as bangers and mash and traditional meat pies.

This drive will greatly enhance a Route 66 adventure. And if you are a fan of scenic drives, this is one you will remember for a lifetime.

ABOVE Built in 1936 to span the East Fork of the San Gabriel River for a highway that was never completed, the Bridge to Nowhere is a popular destination for hikers.

OPPOSITE One of the most beautiful drives in California, Angeles Crest Highway is an engineering marvel that with each mile provides the driver stunning views.

DRIVE FOUR
THE MEGALOPOLIS

MERE WORDS CANNOT ADEQUATELY describe the adventure that is a drive along Route 66 from San Bernardino to Santa Monica. The sites, the history, the gastronomical odyssey, the rich swirl of past, present, and future—they all blend into an invigorating sensory overload.

And Route 66 in the megalopolis is also the gateway to a nearly endless array of attractions. The internationally acclaimed Petersen Automotive Museum is less than eight miles (12.9 km) from the original western terminus of Route 66. And the world-famous farmer's market in Los Angeles, called The Original Farmers Market, is three miles (4.8 km) from Santa Monica Boulevard, Route 66.

We begin our adventure at the junction of Cajon Boulevard, current Route 66, and Kendall Drive, formerly called "City 66," just north of San Bernardino. There is a dark moment in Hollywood history associated with this junction.

It was here on November 19, 1954, that Sammy Davis Jr., returning from Las Vegas, was involved in a horrendous crash. His injuries were serious and resulted in the loss of an eye.

If you follow Kendall Drive, you will continue with North E Street and then west on West 5th Street to Foothill Boulevard. And if Cajon Boulevard is your choice, it connects with North Mount Vernon Avenue and then West 5th Street to Foothill Boulevard.

San Bernardino sets the stage for this adventure. The Mitla Cafe, one family–owned since 1937, at 602 North Mount Vernon Avenue is a Route 66 tradition. The San Bernardino History and Railroad Museum in the beautiful 1918 Santa Fe Depot

preserves the city's rich railroad history. And at the First Original McDonald's Museum located at 1398 N E Street, the entire history of happy meals and the golden arches empire is colorfully preserved.

The drive west along Foothill Boulevard is an almost overwhelming blend of old and new. Strip malls and mini marts are interspersed with vintage neon signage, the remains of old orchards, and revered establishments such as the Wigwam Motel in Rialto that opened in 1950, which make for an unforgettable journey.

Traffic and urban sprawl that has consumed vacant lots as well as farmland become more common with each mile (1.6 km) driven to the west. But salted among modern apart-

BELOW, CLOCKWISE FROM TOP LEFT The distinctly styled Petersen Automotive Museum is one of the world's premier automobile museums with a diverse array of rotating exhibits.

The drive along Route 66 through San Bernardino, Rialto, and west toward Los Angeles is through a swirl of modern suburbia and vintage roadside vestiges.

This garage and service station complex in Rancho Cucamonga dates to the teens but only the station remains as a visitor center and museum.

ment complexes and stores are representations of centuries of history.

A wonderful example is Rancho Cucamonga. This town dates to the establishment of Rancho de Cucamonga in 1839 by Tiburcio Tapía on the site of a Kucamongan tribal village built in about 1200 CE.

At 8318 Foothill Boulevard stands Sycamore Inn that initially opened in 1848. At the end of the parking lot there is a boulevard bridge dated 1936 and an overpass is adorned with a whimsical tribute to Route 66. Located at 8189 Foothill Boulevard is the garishly decorated Magic Lamp Inn restaurant, with its original signage, built in 1955.

Just ten miles (16.1 km) away from the historic Sycamore Inn is the Wally Parks

NHRA Motorsports Museum at 1101 W McKinley Ave. Located on the edge of the Los Angeles County Fairplex, this dynamic museum houses a staggering collection of historic automobiles and motorcycles, memorabilia, and promotional materials that chronicle the history of hot rodding.

Back on Route 66, continue west on Foothill Boulevard through Upland. Here stands the Madonna of the Trail statue. Twelve identical monuments were placed in each of the twelve states along the National Old Trails Road corridor in the 1920s.

The road continues through Claremont, La Verne, San Dimas, Azusa, and Duarte. One of the most challenging aspects of a Route 66 odyssey is avoiding hard braking when you see something amazing and then finding a parking place so you can get a picture or explore.

In Monrovia is the Aztec Hotel at 311 West Foothill Boulevard that opened in 1925. Closed for renovation, the uniquely styled hotel sparked an architectural movement. Many buildings, including the Mayan Hotel in Kansas City, the La Jolla Beach & Yacht Club in La Jolla, and The Mayan Theatre in Los Angeles, were built using the architectural renderings of the Aztec Hotel. There was even a wave of cottage industries manufacturing wall sconces, tiles, and furniture based on designs in the hotel.

At Arcadia, Route 66 followed Huntington Drive and Colorado Place, Colorado Street, and Colorado Boulevard. The celebrated Santa Anita Park and Racetrack and a Dutch-themed Denny's topped with a windmill that is the last survivor of the former Van de Camp's restaurant chain are just a few of the highlights.

The 127-acre (51.4 ha) Los Angeles County Arboretum and Botanic Garden at 301 N Baldwin Avenue in Arcadia is another detour I can recommend. There is a lengthy Hollywood connection with these wonderful gardens. It was here that Hervé Villechaize's character, Tattoo, in the television program *Fantasy Island* rang the bell in the opening scene of the first episodes. Several *Tarzan* movies included scenes filmed here as were scenes in *The African Queen* starring Humphrey Bogart and Katherine Hepburn.

From Pasadena, Route 66 followed several courses into Los Angeles over the years. From 1926 to 1931, it followed Fair Oaks Avenue to Huntington Drive. From 1934 to 1940, the

FROM LEFT Harry Truman was president of the National Old Trails Road Association when the Madonna of the Trail statue was added to the National Old Trails Roadside in Upland.

With its uniquely styled façade, interior, and furnishings, the Aztec Hotel that opened its doors in 1925 spawned an architectural movement.

ARROYO SECO BRIDGE.   PASADENA, CALIFORNIA.

highway continued west on Colorado Boulevard. This alignment served as Alternate 66 from 1940 until 1964.

Urban treasures abound along each alignment. The Colorado Street Bridge that carried Route 66 across Arroyo Seco is an architectural and engineering marvel. Built in 1913, the ornate span stands 150 feet (45.7 m) above the stream bed. At the time of its completion, it was the highest concrete bridge in the world.

On Fair Oaks Avenue, the 1915 Fair Oaks Pharmacy with its soda fountain has become a permanent fixture for locals as well as a popular destination for countless Route 66 enthusiasts.

On December 1, 1940, Route 66 was rerouted over the recently completed nine-mile (14.5 km)-long Arroyo Seco Parkway. This is the only National Scenic Byway that is fully contained in a major metropolitan area.

As an historic side note, with development of the Interstate Highway and Freeway System in Los Angeles, the western terminus of Route 66 was pushed further east. From January 1, 1964, to December 31, 1974, the intersection of the Arroyo Seco Parkway and East Colorado Boulevard was designated the western terminus of that highway.

The original western terminus was at 7th Street and South Broadway, the heart of the city's historic theater district. This gritty, dynamic, fascinating, urban corridor that is deeply shadowed by towering architectural masterpieces is experiencing a slow but dramatic transition.

Lining South Broadway from 3rd to 9th Streets is the historic Broadway Theatre District. Here are twelve theaters, beautiful movie palaces built between 1910 and 1931. At its peak during the 1940s, this district had the highest concentration of theaters in the world. In 1979, the district was added to the National Register of Historic Places.

The Palace Theater opened in 1911 as the Orpheum. On June 26, 2011, for the theater's centennial, it reopened after a million-dollar renovation. The astounding

Los Angeles Theatre had a gala opening on January 30, 1931. Counted among the celebrities that attended a showing of *City Lights* were Charlie Chaplin and Albert Einstein.

The Grand Central Market at 317 South Broadway is an attraction that must be experienced. Housed in the city's first "truly fireproof reinforced steel" multistory building built between 1898 and 1899, the market opened in 1917.

At its opening, it was promoted as the "the largest and finest public market on the Pacific Coast." Today, it is a microcosm of the city's diversity with vendors offering all manner of authentic ethnic foods as well as fresh produce. As a bonus, there is nearly a century of neon signage on display.

Less than a mile (1.6 km) away is the historic Olvera District. A dynamic district of street vendors and festivals, this is the historic heart of Los Angeles. It was here

that El Pueblo de Los Angeles was established in 1781. There are twenty-seven buildings of special interest in the district including the Avila Adobe, the oldest home in Los Angeles built in 1818.

After 1937, the terminus of Route 66 was pushed west along Santa Monica Boulevard to the junction with Highway 101A and Olympic and Lincoln Boulevards in Santa Monica. At various times, it joined with U.S. 101 and the Hollywood Freeway, Hollywood Boulevard, and Sunset Boulevard as Route 66 coursed through Hollywood and Beverly Hills.

As can be imagined, the attractions and sites of note are simply overwhelming in scope as well as diversity. Factor in a few side trips, and you can easily fill multiple holidays.

Some notable locations are the fascinating Hollywood Forever Cemetery founded in 1899; Barney's Beanery at 8447 Santa Monica Boulevard opened in 1927; the astounding

Looking East on Santa Monica Blvd.

CLOCKWISE,
FROM TOP LEFT For
decades the traditional
end of Route 66 is
Santa Monica Pier
with its restaurants,
eclectic shops, and
amusement park.

Several blocks from
the actual western
terminus of Route 66,
this Bob Waldmire
memorial at the end of
Santa Monica Pier is a
fitting end to a magical
journey.

Then and now, the
drive along Santa
Monica Boulevard
stands in stark contrast
to the urban oasis of
Palisades Park over-
looking the dynamic
Santa Monica Pier.

Petersen Automotive Museum at 6060 Wilshire Boulevard; and the Formosa Cafe at 7156 Santa Monica Boulevard in West Hollywood, once a popular hangout for Humphrey Bogart, James Dean, and some of the silver screen's biggest stars.

A few blocks from the western terminus of Route 66 is Palisades Park overlooking the Pacific Ocean and Santa Monica Pier, the traditional end of a Route 66 odyssey. Built in 1909, the pier with its Pacific Palisades Amusement Park, colorful shops, and fascinating restaurants is ideally suited for a celebration.

To wrap up your grand adventure, stop and say howdy to the folks at the Santa Monica Pier Bait & Tackle and Route 66 Gift Shop at the very end of the pier. There is a wonderful photo op in the form of a Route 66 display that is also a tribute to the late Bob Waldmire, an iconic and revered folk artist that made tremendous contributions to the early Route 66 renaissance.

If this journey hasn't sated your hunger for road trip adventure, I have two final side trips to suggest. One is south to El Segundo; and the other is north to Calabasas.

The Zimmerman Automobile Driving Museum at 610 Lairport Street, promoted as "the museum that takes you for a ride" is found with a drive of ten miles (16.1 km) south along Highway 1 to El Segundo. The diverse array of vintage and historic vehicles including street rods and the ice cream parlor is well worth a visit. But what really sets this museum apart is the array of events held at the facility and the Sunday Rides.

Weather permitting, on the second and fourth Sundays of every month, from 10:00 a.m. to 3:30 p.m., visitors are given a ten-minute tour of the surrounding neighborhood from the passenger seat, or rumble seat, of a vintage vehicle. The vehicles used for the rides are selected from the museum collection on a rotating basis.

The second recommended detour is north along Highway 1 that hugs the Pacific coast and then north along Highway 27 and Old Topanga Canyon Road through Topanga State Park and into Calabasas. This delightful twenty-five-mile (40.2 km) drive highlights the unique nature of the Los Angeles metropolitan area.

Even with the crush of traffic in the first few miles (5 to 6 km) of the drive it is difficult not to enjoy the drive framed by towering mountains and classic California beaches. And places like Will Rogers State Beach invite you to slow the pace and simply enjoy the day.

The drive to Topanga and Calabasas is on a twisting narrow highway that climbs through a scenic series of canyons from the beach to nearly one thousand feet (304.8 m) in elevation in the Santa Monica Mountains. Make use of the pullouts to savor the

The diverse array of vehicles at the Automobile Driving Museum, such as this Packard ambulance, is not the only attraction of note at this museum.

scenery that is in stark contrast to the metropolis that is less than twenty-five miles (40.2 km) away.

Calabasas is nestled amongst rolling grassy hills and has a pleasant, inviting atmosphere. As a bit of good advice, if during your LA-area visit there is a need for lodging that won't break the budget, consider this quaint town. As an example, the Good Night Inn consistently receives favorable reviews, and the prices are usually less than $100 per night.

And, it is an ideal place to hang the hat while exploring some of the natural attractions in the area. Established in 1974, the 8,215-acre (3,324.5 ha) Malibu Creek State Park is laced with beautiful trails into Kaslow Natural Preserve, Liberty Canyon, and Udell Gorge.

The Leonis Adobe Museum is a complex complete with blacksmith shop that provides the visitor an opportunity to experience California ranch life in the mid-nineteenth century. The old adobe home listed on the National Register of Historic Places was built in 1844. It remains as one of the oldest surviving homes in the San Fernando Valley.

A drive to Calabasas is an excellent way to wrap up a drive along the Main Street of America. And as our focus with this book has been detours and side trips to enhance the Route 66 adventure, the drive through Topanga Canyon is a fitting end to our odyssey.

Image Credits

A = All, **B** = Bottom, **L** = Left, **M** = Middle, **R** = Right, **T** = Top

Forest Preserve District of Will County: 14BR.

Illinois Department of Natural Resources: 24.

Jax Welborn: 53.

Jim Hinckley's America: 13M, 14L, 15, 16TL, 16ML, 16BL, 17A, 18A, 20L, 20TR, 26TL, 26BL, 27A, 28, 30, 31TR, 31BR, 32TR, 32BR, 33BL, 33TR, 33BR, 34L, 34TR, 35A, 38A, 39BL, 39R, 40, 41B, 42M, 45, 48–49A, 51M, 56, 61M, 62BR, 66–69A, 70, 71, 73TR, 73BL, 74TR, 75T, 75M, 76–77A, 78T, 78TM, 78BM, 80A, 85, 86–87A, 93, 97M, 97B, 98TL, 98TR, 99T, 99M, 100T, 100BL, 101, 104, 108, 110, 111–113A, 115T, 116–118A, 119L, 119BR, 120–124A, 125TL, 125TR, 125BL, 132, 135TL, 135BL, 135BR, 136 –137A, 138TL, 138TR, 139, 140T, 140B, 142TL, 142BL, 144T, 144TM, 144B, 145, 146–147A, 149M, 150L, 150TR, 150BR, 151A, 152, 154BR, 156–159A, 163L, 164B, 165B, 166TL, 166BL, 166TR, 167T, 167B, 168TL, 168B, 169, 170TR, 170BR, 171, 172TL, 172TR, 177A, 178L, 178TR, 178MR, 179A, 180B, 181A, 182B.

Joe Sonderman: 12, 14TR, 22A, 34BR, 36, 39TL, 41M, 42T, 44, 51T, 61T, 79M, 81, 96, 97T, 99B, 162, 163RM, 167T, 178BR.

Judy Hinckley: 19M, 20BR, 33TL, 37, 46, 58, 61B, 62BL, 73BR, 78B, 79T, 98BL, 98BR, 116, 134, 141, 142R, 143, 153, 154TR, 163TR, 163BR, 164TL, 176, 182TR.

Mike Ward: 135TR.

Shutterstock: 2, melissamn; 6TL, Kirk Fisher; 6TR, Keisuke asami; 6ML, Khajohn; 6MR, JeanLuclchard; 6BL, Photos BrianScantlebury; 6BM, Doyne and Margaret Loyd; 6BR, Jacqueline F Cooper; 9, gabriel12; 10, Susan Montgomery; 19B, Everett Collection; 21, Trong Nguyen; 23, James Kirkikis; 25T, Matt Gush; 25M, t. m. urban; 26R, rockolagist; 41T, STLJB; 42B, 4kclips; 43, Andru Goldman; 47, Emily Heart; 50, Jon Manjeot; 52, TommyBrison; 54, Zack Frank; 55, Jacob Boomsma; 57, EWY Media; 64, Everett Collection; 83, Vineyard Perspective; 84, Alizada Studios; 88, James Kirkikis; 90, YuniqueB; 91–92, Richard G Smith; 94, Jacob Boomsma; 102, Connor Belt; 103, Hundley Photography; 105, Bill Hamilton; 107, Jon Manjeot; 126, Stephen B. Goodwin; 127, Kristine Rutledge; 128T, Tami Freed; 129, Eirik Gumeny; 130, Jon Manjeot; 131, Zack Frank; 148, Tim Roberts Photography; 149B, julius fekete; 150RM, Paul McKinnon; 154TL, Melesandre; 154BR, Stephen Moehle; 155M, Jon Marc Lyttle; 155B, jessica. kirsh; 170TL, sumikophoto; 170BL, Steve Cukrov; 172B, AndrePagaPhoto; 173, L.A. Nature Graphics; 174, Noah Sauve; 175, Andy Konieczny; 183, SunflowerMomma; 184 –185, Lando Aviles.

Steve Rider: 13B, 16R, 31L, 32L, 60, 62T, 73TL, 74L, 74BR, 75B, 100BR, 115M, 115B, 119TR, 125BR, 128B, 138B, 140M, 144BM, 160, 164TR, 165T, 165M, 166BR, 168TR, 180M, 182TL.

Index

About the Author

JIM HINCKLEY is the author of twenty books and hundreds of feature articles on Route 66, the American Southwest, and the American auto industry. He has been a featured speaker at European Route 66 festivals in Germany and the Czech Republic, and at events in the United States and Canada. Hinckley is a former associate editor for *Cars & Parts*, and currently writes a monthly feature for New Zealand-based *MotoringNZ*. He also assists with the creation of visitor guides for communities such as Tucumcari, New Mexico, and the development of historic district walking tours. Jim is the creator of the Jim Hinckley's America network that includes a website (jimhinckleysamerica.com/), social media, the weekly livestream "Coffee with Jim" program, a YouTube channel, and the "Wake Up with Jim" podcast. Linked with this are community education programs developed to foster an increased awareness of an area's history and its role in the development of tourism as a component in economic development.